At the Risk of Sounding

ALSO BY LOLA LEMIRE TOSTEVIN

NOVELS

Frog Moon
The Jasmine Man
The Other Sister

POETRY

Color of Her Speech
Gyno-Text
Double Standards
'sophie
Cartouches
Site-Specific Poems
Punctum
Singed Wings

LITERARY CRITICISM

Subject to Criticism

At the Risk of Sounding

ESSAYS BY LOLA LEMIRE TOSTEVIN

Teksteditions
Toronto 2015

Copyright © 2015 by Lola Lemire Tostevin

ALL RIGHTS RESERVED. No part of this book may be reproduced by any means without the prior written permission of the publisher, with the exception of brief passages in reviews. Any request for photocopying or other reprographic copying of any part of this book must be directed in writing to ACCESS Copyright.

Editor: Beverley Daurio

Cover painting: Alice Teichert

Cover concept and colour design: Lola Lemire Tostevin

Cover typography, page design and composition: Beverley Daurio

2015 2016 2017 2018 2019 5 4 3 2 1

First Edition

CiP Data available for this title.

Paperback: 978-1-927367-54-4
Hardcover: 978-1-927367-58-2

Teksteditions
www.teksteditions.com

Persona... originally referred to the actor's mask that covered his individual "personal" face and indicated to the spectator the role and the part of the actor in the play. But in this mask, which was designed and determined by the play, there existed a broad opening at the place of the mouth through which the individual, undisguised voice of the actor could sound. It is from this sounding through that the word *persona* was derived: *per-sonare*, "to sound through..."

—Hannah Arendt
Responsibility and Judgment

Table *of* Contents

A Touch of Evil in Carsairs: The Short Stories of Alice Munro 9

A Difficult Place to Stand:
A Review of *aka bpNichol a preliminary biography* by Frank Davey 19

The Burning Alphabet: The Poetry of Barry Dempster 39

New Configurations for an Old Alphabet: The Art of Barbara Caruso 47

The Error of Their Ways 69

Paule Thévenin 79

Letter to a Friend: Paule Thévenin on Antonin Artaud 83

Florence de Mèredieu: A Review of *L'Affaire Artaud* 101

Mistaken Identity: Plenary Speaking 109

The Art of Alice Teichert in Three Stages 127

Interference: On Reading Lisa Robertson's *Nilling* 153

UnCeremonial Bodies: Nanni Moretti, *We Have a Pope;*
Margarethe von Trotta, *Vision;* Robert Lepage, *Le Confessional* 175

Richard Serra and Kim Ondaatje: *A Matter of Time* 193

What's in a Name? 203

A Touch of Evil in Carsairs:
The Short Stories of Alice Munro

The morning it was announced that Alice Munro had been awarded the Nobel Prize for literature, I overheard, while standing in line at a coffee shop, several men discussing Munro's win. It was surprising and unusual, one of them said, for a woman who writes nice little stories about small towns in Ontario to win such a prestigious prize. It isn't an unusual comment. Alice Munro is often depicted as "a nice little woman who writes nice little stories" by people who have either not read her, or people who have not bothered to scratch the surface of her stories. The most rewarding aspect of doing so is the extent to which she exposes the human condition through seemingly simple, pared-down language. The purity of her style and the succinct narratives of settlers populating small towns and rolling farmlands gradually and ingeniously lift the curtain on secrets, fantasies and, ultimately, the confinement and violence too often found at the heart of unitary communities.

In a combination of third-person and stream-of-consciousness narratives, Munro's stories bring to light what her characters attempt to conceal from others and, more often than not, from themselves. They reveal what is, at times, mean and petty or duplicitous and abject about human nature, even when framed within the idyllic and innocent settings of small, Christian communities. While Munro's stories are told in voices that are on vastly different scales from the mythologies of Typhon, Prometheus, Oedipus or Job, to name but a few, they represent a microcosm of the tragedian history of defilement, guilt and confinement. What is usually consigned to the realm of the inexpressible makes an appearance then withdraws. There is little assurance to be drawn, few lessons to be learned. The absence of such assurance is the touchstone of modernist literature. The communities that once served as models for their simple virtues and traditions can no longer be trusted.

In *Open Secrets* and *Selected Stories*, Munro directs readers away from illusory and ephemeral preoccupations toward her characters' inability to communicate freely or honestly. To give but a few examples, loneliness and regret are never spoken of openly in "Walker Brothers Cowboy," yet everything the characters do or utter points to an underlying hopelessness. The duplicity revealed through Clare's character in "Postcard" is not merely heartbreaking; it is ruthless. The piano teacher, Miss Marsalles of "Dance of the Happy Shades," showcases disadvantaged children in order to maintain the useless ritual of her annual social event. The thoughtless and complacent repetition of habit and tradition play a vital role where the most upright, "most prudish people," in "Royal Beatings," get away with physical abuse of children, even murder. Loneliness, deception, exploitation, abuse and murder are never presented openly but through the mediation of a language that remains virtually silent in its implicitness. Munro never wraps her stories in resolution and precision, the reason perhaps why she has been compared to Chekov.

To reveal evil, or admit to it, goes against most small communities' conventional ways of thinking. Where everyone knows each other's business, the potential relationship with everything that is good, at least on the surface, must be maintained at all cost even if it is, in William Blake's words, of the Devil's party. Submission and obedience to Christian rules (or, for that matter, any religious rules) are always on the side of Good/God. They are revealed through daily activities where the fear of being discovered is presented as compassion, even love. Munro's literary devices expose what her characters try to keep hidden: "The person creating noises in the bathroom is never connected with the person who walked out." Everything must be kept under wraps especially when it comes to the unholy site of the body.

The title story of the collection, *Open Secrets*, is a characteristic example of Munro's literary device. It is a disturbing account of the disappearance of an adolescent girl on an annual hike of the C.G.I.T.—Canadian Girls in Training. One can only wonder what the girls are being trained for exactly. From the first page, the disappearance is treated casually, as not being of any great concern, a mere detail in a story, for had it been raining that day the ritual outing would not have taken place and it would have been "a whole other story." The victim, Heather Bell, a newcomer in town, acted in a way that suggests she may have been asking for whatever fate had in store for her. When the girls stop at a farm and are offered sodas and a hose with which to spray and cool themselves, it is the outsider, Heather Bell, who is described as "the boldest, getting hold of the hose and shooting water on the rest of them in all the bad places." "The bad places" is a metaphor for those adulterated parts of the body that inevitably lead to transgressions. Heather Bell, outsider, may have been little more than a seductress.

Miss Mary Johnstone, who has been leading the hike for more than two decades, always starts off with the girls singing the same song, a prayer-like ritual in praise of the beauty and love of nature—the Earth, the Skies—paeans to the glory of Creation. In Miss Johnstone's mind, earth and sky are connected through their symbolization of what is naturally and morally pure. Residents in the town of Carsairs seldom mention Mary Johnstone without adding how wonderful she is, partly because of her devotion to the girls, partly because she was disfigured by polio as an adolescent, but most importantly because Jesus came to visit her when she was in an iron lung. He might have been dressed as a doctor, but Mary

Johnstone recognized him immediately, and who would dare criticize or question a woman who has had a face-to-face encounter with the Son of God. In His eyes, disfigurement of the body, especially a woman's, is an asset that warrants deference. Unlike Heather Bell's single mother, also an outsider, who wears backless dresses and high heels, or Maureen Stephens, the town lawyer's wife, who is tall and healthy with a rosy complexion, auburn hair and a weakness for stylish clothes. Because they play such important roles in her stories, Munro is very attentive to her characters' physical attributes.

The town places great confidence in Maureen Stephens's husband, Lawyer Stephens, victim of a stroke, whose clothes "never seemed to fit well or to smooth out his long, lumpy body." The town trusts him not only because his head wags downward and his face sags, but also because of his knowledge of the Law. Like Miss Johnstone, his altered physical appearance implies special knowledge, the reason the townspeople come to him for solutions, perhaps even for confession and absolution. They trust him implicitly because their keeper of the Law could have been appointed judge earlier in his career, an appointment he refused on the pretext that he wouldn't "kowtow" to anyone, especially an outsider holding a higher position than his. It seems Lawyer Stephens will not, under any circumstances, put himself in a position he deems servile. In other words, in Carsairs where Lawyer Stephens is the Law, there can be no flexibility of rules carved in the symbolic cornerstone that holds the community together.

When Marian and Theo Slater show up at Lawyer Stephens's house to implicate a Mr. Siddicup in the young girl's disappearance, Maureen Stephens is alerted to what she hears and perceives. Mrs. Slater's appearance, her face overdone with makeup, pale powder hanging from her droopy cheeks, her lips in bright red lipstick, looks almost clownish, a parody of femininity. In exaggerating her features with false makeup, she turns them into false signs. This woman who is "without one visible advantage" may well be trying to hide who she really is. A supposedly upstanding citizen, she is the woman other women go to to be measured for corsets, the rigid undergarments that uphold the body and are worn to modify its natural shape.

The purpose for Mr. and Mrs. Slater's visit is to report an incident involving Mr. Siddicup, who showed up at the Slater farm on the day Heather Bell disappeared. Mr. Siddicup, also an outsider who originally came from England, is mute and unpredictable since undergoing throat surgery for cancer. Since his surgery and his wife's death, he has become a highly suspicious character who deteriorated from a decent man who loved to read and tend his garden into a morose and rather disgusting old vagrant. "Dirty whiskers, dribbles on his clothes, a sour smoky smell" suggest the symbolic stain of sin as it relates to a person's soul and the disfigurement of innocence. The town suspects him to be a pervert given he has his late wife's underwear strewn over his living room and, an even more egregious offense, he is not nearly as grateful as he should be for the charity the town extends him. It is interesting to note that when Mr. Siddicup is seen in a town miles away from Carsairs, his face takes on something of its old expression: "[...] ready for the genial obligatory surprise, the greeting of people who lived in one place meeting in another. It did look as if he had a hope then that the moment would open out, that words would break through, in fact that perhaps the changes would be wiped out, here in a different place [...]. Within the confines of Carsairs Mr. Siddicup is a victim of how he is viewed. Outside Carsairs, he rediscovers traces of his old self, a congenial and independent person.

Because Mr. Siddicup was unable to put into words what he witnessed at the Falls on the Peregrine River, Marian Slater re-enacts, in minute detail, what an agitated Mr. Siddicup purportedly was trying to tell her when he showed up at her door.

It is impossible not to associate the word "Falls" to the original Edenic myth of man's fall, and "Peregrine," to the large predatory bird hunting and killing small prey. Mrs. Slater calls attention to the fact that at the time of Mr. Siddicup's visit she had been in a more or less dream-like state, having taken painkillers for a boil on her neck, as if to emphasize a lack of complete consciousness. The mention of a boil recalls several biblical references to scourges visited on populations as retribution for their sins. It is also important to note that events that cannot be conveyed directly but must be interpreted, as in Mr. Siddicup's case, prove to be the most important in relation to the disappearance of Heather Bell.

Mrs. Slater's husband, an overly deferential man, lets his wife speak for him. During her re-enactment of what Mr. Siddicup supposedly conveyed, she is aware that her husband's eyes are fixed on her by an effort of will, which Maureen Stephens also notices: "Something flashed in his face—a tic, a nerve jumping in one cheek... her look said, Hold on. Be still." As her story develops, the reader learns that it was at the Slaters' farm that the girls stopped for drinks, as described in the first pages. It was at the Slaters' farm that Heather Bell drew attention to herself when Mr. Slater suggested the girls cool themselves down with the hose. It was at the Slaters' farm that Mr. Siddicup showed up, a possible witness unable to tell anyone what he saw, which leaves a blank slate for anyone to fill in.

There is no assurance that Mrs. Slater's story as relayed to Lawyer Stephens is either true or untrue. There is nothing in her rendition to suggest she is lying or that Mr. Siddicup did anything more than convey as best he could what he witnessed. Nor is there anything to indicate she is telling an abridged version or, for that matter, the entire truth. It is from the details around her telling that the reader, through Maureen Stephens, extrapolates what is, or is not, being said. Mr. Slater's deferential manner and his constant apologizing suggest the servility of a guilty person, guilt made manifest as a feeling of unworthiness at the core of his being. When Maureen Stephens describes Mrs. Slater as a woman who presents herself as if she had absolute rights, a woman who had to be taken account of, especially by her husband, the reader is reminded how the imposition of those absolute rights can reduce the person at the receiving end to a life of compliance and servitude. Mr. Slater works as a maintenance man for the Atomic Energy Station, a plant representing supernatural power for which Lawyer Stephens has a great deal of admiration and respect. It is also the kind of work that can alienate man from who he is. Not only can such a supernatural power threaten the whole of mankind, Mr. Slater himself is exposed to high doses of radiation through the x-ray checks he is required to undergo at the end of each day. A man exposed to daily doses of a supernatural power will, eventually, become an altered man. He is a victim of a mutation marked by dissimulation.

Maureen Stephens, who seems to have a more vigilant eye and ear than anyone in Carsairs, does not have complete faith in Mrs. Slater's account. After their visit she watches as the Slaters walk toward the Town Hall and sit on a low stone wall where Mrs. Slater takes out pins from her hat and carefully lifts it off her aching head. She watches as Mr. Slater takes the hat from his wife and strokes its feathers as if he were pacifying a little scared hen, until Mrs. Slater clamps a hand down on his, the way a mother would interrupt a simple-minded child "with a burst of abhorrence, a moment's break in her tired-out love." Through Maureen Stephens, the reader detects a moment of defection on Marian Slater's part. It is an extraordinary moment which does not confirm who killed Heather Bell, yet her simple and unguarded gesture says much more than Mrs. Slater's detailed and re-enacted story. In both cases, actions speak louder than words.

The scene immediately following Mrs. Slater's moment of defection is unexpectedly powerful as it exposes the roots of defilement and evil in the small town of Carsairs. After listening to Mrs. Slater's account, Lawyer Stephens, who usually rejects his young wife's advances with "Now Maureen, what's this all about?" is sexually aroused. There exists a link between the re-enactment around the disappearance of an innocent young girl and the sexual arousal of the keeper of the Law. Each one draws its power from the other. Mrs. Slater's acting out transfers the loss of innocence to Lawyer Stephens who, on one hand, feels his powers have been diminished because of his failure to keep the town within the rules of Law. On the other hand, he is aroused by the accumulation of words and signs around the disappearance of innocence. Where Mr. Siddicup is shocked and feels sullied by what he witnessed at the Falls and seeks to absolve himself by washing at the Slater farm's pump, Lawyer Stephens looks to his wife to regain his powers according to a Law of retribution. In fact, for Lawyer Stephens, listening to a story about possible murder and sexual violation makes the reality of sex more accessible and exciting than shared marital sex. When he commands his wife to "Ta dirty," (talk dirty) during the sexual act, pushing and prodding her, "even trying to jam his fingers into her from behind," the connection between defilement and words brings to light the primordially symbolic representation of everything that is violent and tainted in Carsairs.

A decrease of power is often an open invitation to violence. Those who hold power and feel it slipping from their grasp cannot resist the temptation to substitute it with violence or degradation, or both. The keeper of the Law visits this violence within the confines of his home, on the person closest to him. Having put his wife through a degrading sexual encounter in order to regain his feeling of power, he then refuses to walk with her to the police station to inform on Mr. Siddicup because, ostensibly, being accompanied by a defiled wife would diminish him and the seriousness of his errand. In order to regain his power, the keeper of the Law conforms to the community's prevailing norms.

Unaware and unable to grasp the full reality of what he has heard and done, the would-be judge lacks what is needed to deliver impartial justice: a fully functioning consciousness.

In spite of the lack of evidence tying Mr. Siddicup to Heather Bell's disappearance, the blame nevertheless falls on him. Already branded a "pervert" because of his unkempt appearance, the town collectively decides he should pay a price for violating the town's order: *"He had something to do with it."* The notion of human freedom in Carsairs depends on a strict code of limited behaviour, and under the guise of Preventive Custody Mr. Siddicup is, ironically, committed to the local Mental Health Centre. An unkempt outsider who is unable to speak, in addition to Mr. Siddicup's long list of Job-like misfortunes, all point to some iniquity that must not go unpunished. Whether Mr. Siddicup is guilty of Heather Bell's disappearance and murder becomes irrelevant to the town's notion of righteousness.

Like Mr. Siddicup who has been confined to the Mental Health Centre, each person in Carsairs is, ultimately, captive of an unspoken Law. Whether it is as a symbol of a hen as represented by Mrs. Slater's hat, or the disappearance of Heather Bell, or Maureen Stephens caught in the grips of her husband's demeaning sexual act, each person is a victim of a common setting in the stories of Alice Munro. Like Mr. Siddicup, not only can't the townspeople verbalize the source of the Law by which they live, they are not free to think beyond it. Each person lives according to a tacit decree that holds him or her captive. The power that binds the community to a feeling of subjection holds it as powerfully as if it was caught in a snare. "Evil comes to a man as the 'outside' of freedom, as the other than itself in which freedom is taken captive."

Heather Bell's disappearance and murder is an event for which there is neither meaning nor comfort. On the surface, there is no rhyme or reason for it. Reason, in fact, may well be Carsairs's ultimate foe. Authentic literature may shed light on the Law that prevents individual consciousness but it is hard-pressed to change it. Maureen Stephens's insights may be able to detect the social order at the heart of the community and she may even be able to emancipate herself after the death of her husband and leave Carsairs, but it is not clear whether she will ever successfully escape its imprint.

The subtle yet revolutionary aspect of Alice Munro's writing holds a mirror to characters who never feel remote or contrived. On the contrary, they are familiar and, in many instances, readers may even recognize themselves and their own circumstances. From the particular settings and people of small towns and farms of southern Ontario, Munro is able to convert a subject as abstract and complex as evil and give it cosmic dimensions. It is the reason why this "nice little woman" who writes such "nice little stories" was awarded a Nobel Prize.

WORKS CITED
Munro, Alice. *Open Secrets*. Toronto: McClelland & Stewart, 1997.
_____ *Selected Stories*. Toronto: McClelland & Stewart, 1998.
Ricoeur, Paul. *The Symbolism of Evil*. Trans. Emerson Buchanan. Boston: Beacon Press, 1967.

A Difficult Place to Stand:
A Review of *aka bpNichol a preliminary biography* by Frank Davey (ECW Press, Toronto, 2012)

> I've started to write about writing—& i've found it very good—because it's clarified a lot of things for me —*bpNichol*

Some twenty-eight years ago, I wrote a small piece entitled "Paternal Body as Outlaw" for a collection of essays, *Read the Way He Writes: A Festschrift for bpNichol*. It *was* an exciting time to be writing, especially for women who were challenging conventional and traditional forms and questioning assumptions that defined what "a woman" should be. We explored new themes and forms; some women bolstered these with various theories, some preferred not to, although most of us were often herded as either "language" or "experimental" writers. I, personally, never fully understood the term "experimental." Few writers think of their writing as "experimentation." Nor have I ever understood the rigid line drawn between so-called "language" and "non-language" writers.

Through fundamental questioning of the past, women and men were injecting new vitality into their literary texts. It was important that their voices be voices of difference, a concept often identified as a feminine economy of language, or, as French theorists called it, *écriture féminine*, until it too was marginalized and branded either as essentialist or overly influenced by a male elite. Faced with so much dissension, some women found solace and strength within intimate and protective communities, until the creative imagination, in striving to set itself free from one set of limits, could no longer remain indifferent to new ones. Writing, regardless of form or content, was not the exclusive right of any one group. Women and men were exploring untraditional forms and challenging the definition of legitimate literature. Canada had its own upstarts and what better example than the performance group of The Four Horsemen? What better example than the anchor of the group—as everyone secretly acknowledged—bpNichol? As he wrote at the beginning of *The Martyrology Book I*, "so many bad beginnings / you promise yourself / you won't start there again." And a few pages later, "the hierarchy's a difficult place to stand."

There is a strong sense of history throughout Nichol's work, but the story behind the history is of the writer at the moment of writing where "feeling / knowing the words are/ i am" (Book I). In breaking away from prescriptive rules traditionally identified with the authoritative figure of the father, the son channels himself through his own, innovative forms. Nichol's use of hierarchical terms such as *The Martyrology*, "Book of Common Prayer," "Book of Hours," are not retrievals of religious history, but a retrieval of the mood of chants and incantation that draw upon language's most communicative rhythms. His songs, word-play, puns, and games (such as making up the names of saints from words that start with "st") emphasize a departure from mythical saints and embrace an unsanctified devoutness to the primacy of language. A literary conversion if you will, a symbolic event leading the writer toward self-definition and significance. Which brings me to the recently published *aka bpNichol a preliminary biography* by Frank Davey.

I wondered at the use of "preliminary" in the title. Was this meant as an incomplete biography, an introductory, preliminary sketch that would eventually lead to a fuller portrayal? It reminded me of Nichol's *The True Eventual Story of Billy the Kid*, one of the many metaphoric personas Nichol adopted in his creation of stories. Facts about Billy the Kid's life are scant but the story grows with time as all stories are apt to. Was this what Davey envisaged, a true eventual "story" of Nichol? Many of Davey's inferences and interpretations are couched with qualifiers such as "presumably," "quite possibly, " "probably," "seems likely," "most likely," "hints of," "suggests that," "perhaps because," and so on. It isn't long into the book before it conveys less of a legendary tone and more of unsubstantiated gossip.

Davey bases his biography on the postulation that there were mainly two Nichols—Barrie Nichol, his life outside writing, including his early years as a writer—and bpNichol, his life in writing, the latter a signature that he adopted as an alternative to the many personas he used while deploying an expanding number of genres. Much of the book revolves around attempts to negotiate a passage of legitimacy between Nichol's private life (Barrie) and his written life (bp). Anyone who has read Nichol is aware of his multiple doublings, the elusive identities that refuse to be pinned down into a singular "I" or, for that matter, merely two of them. Nichol's use of the title *The Martyrology* for his life-long poem reflects his need to deflect, even sacrifice, the ego, or what he often referred to as the writer's "arrogance" or "narcissism."

Few writers believe that autobiography or biography offer faithful reconstructions of a historically verifiable past. Most understand the differences among the remembered, the imagined, and the written lives. Most are aware that in writing, memory is retrieved and staged for different intents or genres—story, poetry, diary/journal, drama, performance, children's literature, chants, songs, opera, comics, visual art... all of which Nichol explored during his twenty-five years or so as a writer.

Davey's Introduction is headed by a Henry Miller quotation Davey found in one of Nichol's notebooks, "Houses of the Alphabet," taken from Jay Martin's biography *Always Merry and Bright:*

I am highly suspicious of well-documented biographies, just as I am skeptical about historical records and events. If on the other hand, the biographer would write about his subject purely from his imagination, from what he thinks the subject was or is, that is another matter.

It would seem that Davey uses this quotation to justify whatever he *imagines* about his subject; however, the quotation misleads in at least two ways. The entire quotation in Martin's biography ends with the following: "It's this business of writing as if [the biographer] knew all about the subject that bothers me." According to Miller, "biographers are mistaken when they think they know an author by reading his letters, meeting his friends, picking up scraps of one sort or another here, there, everywhere." Miller makes it clear that he doesn't regard what a biographer writes "from his imagination" as representing a true or even relevant image of his subject. In addition, Davey doesn't tell the reader that the Miller quotation is part of an idea Nichol had for a game or novel based both on the Miller quotation and a Ludwig Wittgenstein concept. I believe that Nichol had read an early edition of a biography of Wittgenstein by Norman Malcolm, *Ludwig Wittgenstein: A Memoir,* at about the same time he read the Miller biography. The Wittgenstein biography gives several examples of how Wittgenstein thought of philosophy as consisting of jokes and games. Many sources, including Steve McCaffery's and bpNichol's *Rational Geomancy: The Kids of the Book-Machine: The Collected Research Reports of the Toronto Research Group*, have indicated that Nichol was influenced by Wittgenstein's investigations emphasizing variable uses of language as substitutes for orthodoxy. Nichol was also influenced by Wittgenstein's interpretation of philosophical problems as puzzles that do not necessarily lead to definitive answers.

I'm not pretending to understand Nichol's exact intentions in the two notebook pages in question, but it's evident that whatever he was planning was more complex than simply sanctioning a biographer's imagination. The first notebook page has drawings of proposed front and back book covers. The front cover bears the number 252, whose significance I'm not aware of. The back cover bears Wittgenstein's name. This is followed by rules of a "game" and notes "for Novel." He "plays" with algebraic equations using an unknown factor of "x" multiplied by "changes" inside brackets. This is followed by the Miller quotation but also by Nichol's own words: "different operators could be reading different books, performing different functions and could be reading (a) biog of a bpNichol." On the second page he again identifies "x" as "the structure," then draws a slash down the middle of "x" to form *— an asterisk. In historical linguistics, an asterisk indicates that a symbol has been reconstructed on the basis of linguistic material. In programming language, the asterisk is used to refer to aliases or variables on a given name, all of which played important roles in Nichol's writing. He is clearly suggesting that basic structures are changed according to different readings and "operators." The variable "x" becomes other than the original, perhaps an asterisk, maybe a star, or even a footnote. In another notebook quoted in *Rational Geomancy,* Nichol writes:

> [H]istory (is) simply a way of making a particular sequence "meaningful..." [I]f you go far enough back or far enough forward in time you step outside of it—you are less & less tied to verisimilitude because there is no "reality" to oppose your "Fiction."

Davey claims both in his Introduction and at the end of his biography that Nichol would have wanted his writing to be read as autobiography. It is unlikely that Nichol meant traditional or prescribed concepts of "autobiography." Having been influenced by Gertrude Stein's own autobiographical writing, he was aware of the creation of a self as an art/fact exploring a process of consciousness for both writer and reader. *Art facts: a book of contexts,* was the name of a manuscript that Nichol sent to Chax Press in Tucson, Arizona, which was published posthumously in 1990. Both Stein and Nichol wrote extensively on the *artifact*, the art/i/fact of the self. Both understood that where biography is likely to delve deeper into what is presented in a traditional autobiography, it cannot delve deeper, *biographically,* into a work of art or an art/fact. Biography can analyze the merits of a work of art, it can theorize, and intellectualize, but, as regards any relevant biographical information, it can only presume or construe. There is no reliable synthesis between biographical information and a poem, for example. Each is developed on a different plane and, more often than not, each travels in opposite directions. A work of art doesn't lead to "true" biographical fact any more than biography leads to the true meaning of a work of art. Martin's biography of Miller ends with the following:

> Miller wasn't much happier with those supposedly responsible, serious university critics who sought to put him in what they regarded as his proper place… Even more he found that critics now possessed an annoying tendency to think their own thought … The problem was that he had created a Henry Miller, which for him, was the true Miller…

Nichol created a bpNichol whose history was "literalized," which, as far as he was concerned, was the true Nichol. Writing, for Nichol, was a mix of truth as fiction and fiction as truth. To ignore this is to negate the constructs of Nichol's literary games, in which the reader is invited to participate. Throughout his biography, Davey emphasizes Nichol's fascination with variability and his multiple self-constructed identities, his semi-fictional versions, yet he insists on establishing a binding synthesis between the private life of Barrie Nichol and the writer, bpNichol. He purports to uncover, through notebooks, letters, and what Miller calls "scraps" of one sort or another, autobiographical "truth," whereas Nichol's art exceeds "truth" within a genre that would best be described as *autofiction*. For example, Nichol's novel, *Journal*, implies a record-keeping activity, but the usual definition of "journal" is displaced as the text maintains a vertiginous performative act described by Stephen Scobie in *bpNichol: What History Teaches* as a "sequence of events broken up, rearranged, overlapped, repeated, to prevent the reader from getting caught up in the seriality of a story." Davey refers to *Journal* as a *nouveau roman*, a genre that subordinates plot and character to objects and details of a visual world. *Journal* does subordinate plot, but in its dreamy stream-of-consciousness the narrator is featured as being split between "I" and "he." The novel presents an emotional rollercoaster of narrator(s)—child and young adult facing loss— loss of childhood, separation from (m)other—not merely separation from the personal mother as Davey implies, but the frustration of a subject who must accept that he is no longer the centre of an other's attention, including that of several ex-lovers. It captures the emotional conflict that arises from failed love, and anger at the hierarchy represented by the name of the "father." Again, this does not imply simply the familial father, but the authoritative social order traditionally represented by patriarchy. The narrator/dreamer of *Journal* yearns for the tenderness and innocence of childhood as depicted in the last section of the "journal" when the child "no higher than [his mother's] waist dances with her." A few lines from the end of his "journal," the adult narrator writes: "... when you put this book down I won't be there," thus emphasizing that events are happening within the performative act of writing. Both Scobie and Davey describe the book as Oedipal desire on the part of the dreamer/writer, although Scobie believes the novel moves through and beyond the Oedipal. Davey wonders if, according to a Nichol notebook, the dancing recollections aren't "fantasies or descriptions of innocent scenes." He also speculates they "might" have happened at a specific address during a specific time in Nichol's childhood and adds that this "isn't clear" (30). Immediately, on the next page, he describes how these possible innocent fantasies taken from the notebook have been transcribed in *Journal* as "lurid and hallucinatory passages of Oedipal desire ... [which] offer even stronger hints of why Barrie's teenage years would be so tumultuous" (31). Once again he tries to establish a binding correlation between fantasies or innocent scenarios and a piece of creative writing described as "lurid," a word Davey uses more than once.

Having read *Journal* several times, I must admit it never occurred to me to distill its meaning to instances of Oedipal desire. Yes, the novel yearns for innocence and bonds of affection that exist within all but the most troubled families, but this novel's family far exceeds the personal family. It is within the family of humankind that the split narrators are trying to find a place. The worst that can be said about *Journal* is that it is very dramatic and all women are portrayed as incarnations of a single life-force, women as Woman. This and the difficult transition from family to autonomy are not unusual in the work of young writers. Many find resolution in the recreation of a world through writing, as Nichol did. Where Davey, via Freud, suggests that much of Nichol's unhappiness stemmed from an unhappy childhood due to Oedipal feelings, I detect an attempt to sensationalize what seems to be a pretty normal family in its imperfection. In reading Davey, it's as if from the age of two Nichol had been at the mercy of perpetual childhood.

There are interesting aspects to Davey's book, such as the history of writing and writers during the sixties and seventies.

There is also ample evidence Davey admired bpNichol and his many talents. As already intimated, however, I find one aspect of the book extremely problematic, namely, Davey's persistent allusions to Freudian concepts, especially the Oedipal, to explain Nichol's various relationships. Davey not only assigns the Oedipal to Nichol's real-life mother and, by association, to his father, but also to women Nichol's own age who, according to Davey, also awoke "old Oedipal feelings." Davey returns to Freudian scenarios so often that I wondered if he wasn't affected by what Freud calls "the compulsion to repeat." For Freud, repetition is a means of lending energy to what could otherwise remain imperceptible. Gertrude Stein uses repetition in her writing for similar reasons, as does Nichol. I often wondered if this was also Davey's strategy, compulsively repeating to better unveil what he interprets as the imperceptible in Nichol's work. Lines or segments from poems cited by Davey as proofs of his premises are sometimes so forced it's as if he were trying to make Nichol's writing fit his own preconceived ideas. For example, the line from *The Martyrology, Book II* in the "Auguries" passages, "she is a ghost who walks among my feelings," is, according to Davey, "probably" Barrie's mother and "probably" refers to his increasing Freudian insights into his "unhealthy relationship with her." He follows this by asking if Nichol was "recognizing the Oedipal trap he was in." One is tempted to ask, "Does Davey?" He then adds that although Nichol's reflections were pointing that way, they were in no way "*explicit*" (my italics).

Another example of how Davey tries to synthesize what he perceives as biographical material and poetry is his interpretation of a poem from Chain 3 of *The Martyrology, Book 5*. The poem is offered as evidence that at the age of "three or six or eight months of age," Nichol might have tried to commit suicide, but ultimately chose to live:

My sister Donna died
six weeks old
as i almost died
six months old
Rupert Street in Vancouver
choking to death for no reason
the no reason was inside me

Davey then "clarifies" this poem by writing that Nichol got his sister's and possibly his own age correct, but got the place of his near-death wrong. This is akin to saying that a detail from a painting, say a Picasso, is wrong because an eye is not realistically positioned. Davey's reading of this poem echoes Freud's habit of providing his own hypotheses and theoretical speculations to substantiate what his patients were not telling him. Davey writes, "Words are not to be taken at face value," yet he expects readers to take him at his word.

Theories and hypotheses are as relevant as they are made to be in one's own time and culture. Freud, as much as he believed he had transcended puritanical Victorian mores, never did. Suggestions of sexual behaviour or deviation were sources of scandal and titillation in Vienna in the early part of the twentieth century, which made Freud's psychoanalytical theories quite popular. The more Freudian language was used around sexual issues, and the more logic it supposedly embodied, the more it reached the hypothetical regions of the true "self." By postulating the existence of the subconscious—admittedly a brilliant postulation—Freud stumbled upon a way of presenting it on an empirical and scientific basis. This placed him in a position where he could supply evidence to substantiate any theory he formulated. Freud's biographer, Ernest Jones, introduced the Oedipus complex as the breakthrough that allowed Freud to escape from the tyranny of his (failed) seduction theory, a theory that seriously implicated young women and their fathers. Freud, according to Jones, eventually recognized that his father was innocent of everything of which he had accused him and admitted he had projected onto him ideas of his own. As to Freud's mother and the Oedipal complex, Jones goes on to say that Freud admitted he never actually saw his mother naked as he had claimed when positing his Oedipal theory and that he was engaging in characteristic psychoanalytic activity of "empiricizing" something that had not been part of his experience at all. According to Jones, less than two weeks after confiding this artificially reconstructed memory to his friend Wilhelm Fliess, Freud used it as the basis for a universal law—not a law restricted to Victorian and puritanical mores in Austria, but a universal law according to which all boys, from the age of two to three, feel pleasurable sensations in their penis and fantasize becoming their mother's lover. Two- and three-year-olds seek to replace their fathers' role by plotting to get rid of him, until such time as they eventually identify with the father and seek sexual satisfaction elsewhere. As many critics of Freud have noted, including Ernest Jones and Richard Webster (the controversial author of *Why Freud Was Wrong*) his writings give considerably more attention to infantile sexuality than to its mature expression.

According to Webster, Freud tended to become trapped within the logic of his own theories. (One of my favourites is how children make the imaginative equation between babies and faeces.) He had, in his "penis-envy" phase, come up with the theory that, for a woman, a baby is a replacement for the much-envied penis, but he also tried to establish an organic equation between penis and faeces, disregarding the fact that, according to his own logic, the mother's nipple and the child's thumb had prior claims to that same penis. In view of all this, Freud established a theory of correspondences in which penis, baby, faeces, nipple, and thumb are equivalent and can replace one another freely. In order to protect these great insights, Freud maintained that his theories were not accessible and intelligible to those who were not trained in psychoanalysis, an attitude I personally encountered during my two years of private and group therapy at Therafields. Freud did not recognize women's justification in questioning Freudian interpretations that implicate mothers and women. Once, when I brought up a similar concern during a group session of ten or so people, only Nichol came to my defense. As Betty Friedan pointed out in the early sixties, Freudian thought led men and women to misinterpret their mothers' frustrations, their fathers' resentments, and even their own emotions and choices.

What is so frustrating and sad about Oedipal reasoning is how it fails to encompass one of the most intense and complex of all human relationships, that of a child and its *nurturing* caregivers, especially the mother. It's as if multifaceted emotional and nurturing relationships had to be suppressed and reduced to a two-year-old's penile sensations. Oedipal reasoning robs men of emotional complexity, a quality I never found lacking in Nichol's writing.

Davey's reliance on Freudian hypotheses is a surprising strategy considering so many have been questioned, if not entirely discredited. Given Freud's views on various matters, such as the hysterical female, his seduction theory, and his notion of penis-envy, it is difficult to take his theory of infantile sexuality seriously. Yet, according to Davey, even songs Nichol wrote as a mature adult for a musical revue, *Group: a theradramatic musical,* carry undertones of Oedipal angst: "Australopithecus" Davey writes, is about family transferences; "Ordinary Man" is about psychic masochism; "Great Men Sleep til Noon" is about narcissism, and "I Am Obsessed with My Mother's Breasts" is about the persistence of Oedipal desire. To which he adds that insiders who knew something of Nichol's past—including Davey, of course—had additional reason to laugh. I saw *Group* at least twice and I remember laughing hilariously, not because I "knew of something in Nichol's past," but because the play was so obviously satirical.

Satire pokes sardonic humour at subjects, ideas, or institutions in order to be critical in a self-knowledgeable way. *Group* achieves this through humour and wit. Wit, in fact, played an important role in Nichol's writing, as it did in his everyday life. It served as another example of wordplay that breaks down social inhibition, just as his habitual telling of groaningly bad jokes at dinner parties or breaking into song in public. Challenging social convention and the Establishment is what Nichol did. Davey briefly touches on this side of Nichol's personality, but merely as an aside.

Nichol's language is perhaps at its wittiest in *Organ Music*, which, yet again, Davey claims is "most likely related to Nichol's Oedipal preoccupations." Nichol's exploration of various parts of the body in *Organ Music* explores the relationship between the inside and the outside of the body through language. If we were to compare Nichol's writing to the Freudian sexual paradigm, as Davey insists on doing, it would be less phallic in the usual tradition of pen/penis as fetish and less historically Oedipal since the mother's body, "The Vagina"—the first poem of the book—is presented as birthplace, as entrance into the world. It is an entrance that reaches beyond the phallic order of language. In fact, the phallus/penis in *Organ Music* is referred to as "The Lily," hardly an image that conveys the power of a phallic order. Wit, when used as an aesthetic, is a means of access to usually socially repressed subjects—such as "the vagina," "the anus," "the lily." *Organ Music* not only defies the normally unacceptable; it outwits it.

Few subjects remain untouched in Nichol's writing: son, friend, lover, husband, father constantly offer new chains intersecting with the physical, the temporal, and the textual. The birth/death cycle he shares with his wife, Ellie, in the powerful "Hour 13" in "The Book of Hours" (*Martyrology, book 6*) doesn't simply depict a real-life experience of gestation, birth, death of a son when "briefly / the heart does break"; it underlines the extraordinary impact of language's restorative power.

For all his speculations, Davey provides few reliable details of Nichol's years of therapy at Therafields since all their records were destroyed. Nor do readers interested in Nichol's literary work need to know details of his therapy. In the intermediary world where writing and history mingle, plasticity should be achieved without the reader needing to know where the principle of this malleability lies. It is certainly plausible that therapy freed Nichol to write. There's little doubt, according to his dedications of the first five books of *The Martyrology*, that he was indebted to his therapist, Lea Hindley-Smith, for being a catalyst through which he explored his many voices as a writer. It's possible, from Nichol's notebooks, to conclude that he may have struggled with certain issues, but I would be wary of issues couched in Freudian suppositions. It isn't unusual for therapists to seek out hypothetical traumatic experiences and to create false memories of those experiences. I'm not saying this happened at Therafields, nor am I saying it couldn't have happened. Davey points out that "the mark of a successful therapy is the extent to which the patient has internalized the therapist and begun asking oneself questions similar to those the therapist has posed." In other words, therapy is deemed successful to the extent a patient lets himself be directed by the therapist. Similarly, would Davey's biography be deemed successful to the extent a reader lets himself be directed by Davey's reading of Nichol?

Davey claims that *The Martyrology* is "the epic life-journey of a psychoanalysis ... as Freud had written in 1937 ... the ongoing history of a modernism founded in Freud and Darwin and elaborated by Stein ..." A page later, he admits Nichol might have transcended the dominant international aesthetic of his period, mainly postmodernism. I suspect that in much of his writing Nichol had also transcended the 1937 Freud. Especially if he had read a 1945 letter written by Wittgenstein as it appears in Norman Malcolm's memoir:

I, too, was greatly impressed when I first read Freud.... Of course he is full of fishy thinking & his charm & the charm of the subject is so great that you may easily be fooled. He always stresses what great forces in the mind, what strong prejudices work against the idea of psychoanalysis. But he never says what an enormous charm that idea has for people, just as it has for Freud himself... Unless you think *very* clearly psychoanalysis is a dangerous & a Foul practice & it's done no end of harm &, comparatively, very little good.

On the same subject, Wittgenstein warns Malcolm to "hold on to your brains." The self-knowledge Nichol acquired over the years came mainly from the production of his art. According to the French philosopher Jean-Luc Nancy in *The Birth to Presence*, Freud himself admitted not knowing how to penetrate the creative mind, and art was a gift that remained inaccessible to analysis.

I'm reminded of a conversation I had with Nichol around 1981 when he would have been thirty-seven years old. He was editing my first collection of poems, *Color of Her Speech*, for Coach House Press. Because the book had been written partly during the year I attended a writers' group overseen by Nichol and Grant Goodbrand at Therafields, I had acknowledged this at the end of the book. Barrie suggested I keep his and Goodbrand's names, but was adamant about removing "Therafields." The conversation subsequently turned to psychotherapy. I distinctly remember him saying it was sometimes necessary to go through a process in order to get beyond it. I came across a similar comment by Julia Kristeva some fifteen years later in an interview on the subject of psychoanalysis: "We may need to move beyond that work, but in doing so we have to pass *through* it"—Kristeva's italics. Oh, that Beep, I thought, always ahead of the game. His interest in Wittgenstein also indicates he was ahead of most in language games. In Malcolm's memoir, a mutual friend and colleague of

Wittgenstein at Cambridge, George Henrik von Wright, is quoted: "Wittgenstein felt he was writing for people who would think a different way, breathe a different air of life from that of the present-day men." I am not trying to make Nichol appear flawless or greater than he was, but there is no doubt he thought differently and processed those thoughts into original art forms. To paraphrase Scobie, Nichol's originality and creative language do not report reality, they create it.

A review by David Staines in the *Globe and Mail* on Saturday, 3 November 2012, suggests that Davey's book will be a great asset to those who study or read Nichol in the future. I would urge those students or readers not to frame their readings with Davey's biography. Nichol's writing is far from lifeless, yet if you let Davey's analysis creep into your reading you will soon feel the joy and inventiveness weighed down by speculation and pseudo-Freudian gloss. I tried to imagine what would happen to those extraordinary scenes in Proust's *In Search of Lost Time* when the child anticipates his mother's visits to kiss him goodnight if the reader immediately branded those scenes as Oedipal. Proust's astonishing form and language in those particular passages would suddenly take on very different connotations, and the emotional complexity between child and mother would be lost. What would happen if we were to apply Davey's various modifiers such as "lurid," "vulgarly," "chilling," and so on to Proust, as he's done to Nichol?

For people who knew Barrie as a friend, the grief immediately following his sudden death was all-consuming. We mourned until it was thought best to relinquish the mourning to his wife, Ellie, and his daughter, Sarah.

For those who knew and appreciated Nichol mainly as a writer, the memories were and should continue to be of his writing. It is within this autofictive space created by the many names of bpNichol that readers will encounter a multi-talented writer and innovative thinker. For those who do not know of Nichol's art I would encourage them to read *The Martyrology*, but should they feel intimidated by its nine books, I recommend they ease their way with samples of Nichol's other work as in *An H in the Heart, A Reader*, published by McClelland & Stewart as part of their Modern Canadian Poets Series. It features the many talents of Nichol as poet, maker of music, visual and conceptual artist, and more. Davey tries to make the case that Nichol wouldn't have wanted to be published by such a large publisher as M&S and quotes Steve McCaffery on the issue. Nichol himself had obviously changed his mind on this matter since one of his children's books, *Once a Lullaby*, illustrated by the well-known illustrator, Anita Lobel, was published in 1986, two years before his death, by a large American company, Greenwillow Books, a division of William Morrow & Co. Davey's statement does raise the question, however: would Nichol have wanted his life and body of work interpreted according to Davey's paradigm? Nichol, as part of the Canadian literary canon, achieved a far-reaching national and international reputation, and it is appropriate that he should be recognized by both small and larger presses. Nichol trusted his wife Ellie implicitly—the reason he named her as his literary executor. As such, she was fully justified in giving two of Nichol's good friends, George Bowering and Michael Ondaatje, permission to edit *An H in the Heart* for M&S. Its contents, the Introduction by Bowering and the Afterword by Ondaatje, capture the essence of Barrie, bp, and a multitude of names adopted by Nichol during his too-brief career.

Davey mentions several times that Ellie Nichol, after reading the first draft of his manuscript, refused him permission to quote material from Nichol's archives and published material. In this she was also justified. As executor of his will, she has the right to protect her husband's legacy as she sees fit.

I've had reason to be thankful to Frank Davey over the years. He invited me to teach creative writing at York University when he was Chair of the English Department; he also invited me to serve as Writer-in-Residence at the University of Western Ontario when he was Carl F. Klinck Chair in Canadian Literature; he has given me the opportunity to edit a few issues of *Open Letter*. For this I am indeed thankful. I looked forward to reading his book on Nichol and told him so. After reading it, I had occasion to tell him I sympathized with Ellie Nichol's objections. He answered that perhaps I would have preferred if he hadn't written a book at all. Well ... I wish it had been a different book. I wish, in recognizing Nichol's talent as one of the most innovative Canadian writers of his generation, which endures to this day, Davey had offered more concrete evidence of who Nichol was in his everyday life and as a writer instead of consistently trying to make him and his work fit old and tired Freudian clichés.

WORKS CITED

Jones, Ernest. *The Life and Work of Sigmund Freud: Vol. 1*. New York: Basic Books, 1953.

Kristeva, Julia, and Vassiliki Kolocotroni. *Julia Kristeva Interviews*. Ed. Ross Mitchell Guberman. New York: Columbia UP, 1996.

Malcolm, Norman. *Ludwig Wittgenstein: A Memoir*. Oxford: Oxford UP, 1984.

Martin, Jay. *Always Merry and Bright: The Life of Henry Miller*. New York: Penguin Books, 1980.

McCaffery, Steve and bpNichol. *Rational Geomancy: The Kids of the Book Machine: The Collected Research Reports of the Toronto Research Group 1973-1982*. Ed. Steve McCaffery. Vancouver: Talonbooks, 1992.

Nancy, Jean-Luc. *The Birth to Presence*. Trans. Brian Holmes and others. Stanford: Stanford UP, 1993.

Nichol, bp. *Art Facts: A Book of Contexts*. Tucson: Chax Press, 1990.

———. *An H in the Heart: A Reader*. Ed. George Bowering and Michael Ondaatje. Toronto: McClelland & Stewart, 1994.

———. *Journal*. Toronto: Coach House Press, 1978.

———. *The Martyrology, Book I*. Toronto: Coach House Press, 1972.

———. *The Martyrology, Book II*. Toronto: Coach House Press, 1972.

———. *The Martyrology, Book 3 & 4*. Toronto: Coach House Press, 1976.
———. *The Martyrology, Book 5*. Toronto: Coach House Press, 1982.
———. *The Martyrology, Book 6*. Toronto: Coach House Press, 1987.
———. *Organ Music*. Windsor: Black Moss Press, 2012.
———. *The True Eventual Story of Billy the Kid*. Toronto: Weed/Flower Press, 1970.
Scobie, Stephen. *bpNichol: What History Teaches*. Vancouver: Talonbooks, 1984.
Tostevin, Lola Lemire. "Paternal Body as Outlaw." *Read the Way He Writes: A Festschrift for bpNichol*. Ed. Paul Dutton & Steven Smith. *Open Letter*, Sixth Series, Nos. 5-6 (Summer-Fall 1986).
Webster, Richard. *Why Freud Was Wrong*. New York: Basic Books, 1995.

(Note: For more than thirty years I had on my shelves *The Standard Edition of the Complete Psychological Works of Sigmund Freud, London: Hogarth Press, 1956-1974*. A few years ago, not anticipating I would ever need to write on Freud, I gave the books away. I've relied, therefore, mainly on secondary sources when referring to some of his theories. For more general comments I've relied on memory.)

The Burning Alphabet:
The Poetry of Barry Dempster
(Brick Books, London, 2005)

When I was asked to give a paper on Barry Dempster's *The Burning Alphabet*,* I decided I would not bring to my reading any preconceived or predetermined ideas around lyrical poetry, at least inasmuch as this is possible. In choosing to read only the kind of poetry defined by categories, readers often miss out on work that could expand their knowledge.

The first poem of *The Burning Alphabet*, "Explicit," is an ode to the embodiment of moments as concrete as a heartbeat that "billows a Niagara of the blood." It is a great image, but it is, nevertheless, a metaphoric image. From the very first poem, Demptster's writing divides itself. On one hand, the speaker claims to cherish, above all, the explicit, which, by definition, should express unambiguously what is meant. On the other hand, the heartbeat is described as a larger-than-life image. Is it, therefore, explicit?

Why does the speaker of this poem cherish the explicit? Because, he claims, those who love ambiguity dissolve and disappear. They die quietly and are forgotten. Ironically—irony plays an important part in this collection—as explicit as the

---

* An early version of this essay was presented to a class at the University of Toronto School of Continuing Studies overseen by Margaret Christakos—Influency: A Toronto Poetry Salon. At each session, seven poets from a diverse field of poetics were invited to participate as readers and critics over a seven-week period. Each poet was paired with another from the group and prepared a lecture on the work of that particular poet.

speaker of these poems wants to be, poetry remains ambiguous when things, such as the heart, remain invisible and must be represented by metaphor. The poem is split much as the speaker of the poem in "Suburban Poet" is split. The man who lives with the demands of everyday life and who is addressed as "you," is also the poet who is addressed as "he." It reminds me of the split Virginia Woolf spoke of when she said that when she was with friends, she was Virginia Woolf, but when she wrote she was merely sensibility.

In the second poem, "Handprints," the speaker finds himself scrunched inside a womb-like cave where it is warm and damp "as if corpses had started to breathe again." "As if" is a conditional clause since the corpses aren't there. Yet, because of handprints on the wall, the cave becomes a potentially re-active space where someone from the distant past reaches out and touches the speaker of the poem. The handprint becomes a "touchstone" where the dead are given a new but different kind of life. A death/re-birth image. The traces left behind offer the writer the possibility of cohabiting, of having an exchange, with the past. To paraphrase André Malraux in *The Voices of Silence*, death cannot still the voice. It triumphs over death by compelling us to listen to language as if it were an echo answering each passing century with its own voice, a dialogue undefeated by Time.

It's often said that loss functions as the organizing principle in life, and loss plays a significant role in *The Burning Alphabet*. Death, loss of health, loss of time appear and reappear in the repetitions of everyday events, familiar despairs. Loss underlies the speaker's efforts to represent everyday reality with the cumulative effect of emphasizing the void at the core of a life that is slipping away. There is, in fact, a very tangible sense of time passing in this book. As Hannah Arendt has pointed out in much of her writing, man is not just temporal; he is Time. The speaker of these poems is not only temporal, he is Time passing, he is himself the matter of time. With his own eventual passing, as with his father's passing, there will be no time except in the traces, the handprints, the writing left behind.

Since the beginning of representation, whether through handprints in caves or Egyptian hieroglyphs, loss and representation have been connected. Ancient Egyptian monuments and artifacts are well-known evidence of a culture's preoccupation with the dead and writing. The Egyptians invented writing to take the place of those who were no longer amongst them. In Ancient Egypt's *The Book of the Dead,* the heart is represented by an inkwell in the shape of a heart.

No one understood the connection between loss and writing better than the writers quoted by Dempster at the beginning of each poem in the section "Sick Days," each quote an intertextual exchange that echoes the ideas of each writer's work. The quote from Roland Barthes defines an image as something from which the "I" is excluded, an image where the real person becomes a void. Walter Benjamin's quote conveys loss as a "separation [that] penetrates the disappearing person like a pigment and steeps him in gentle radiance." Pablo Neruda's radiance, on the other hand, glows into "a burning alphabet." The speaker of Dempster's poems, however, isn't settling for gentle radiance; he has decided to go down in flames.

I was intrigued by this collection's title and the cover image. Why the incendiary title and why Betty Goodwin's painting, *Moving Towards Fire?* Goodwin is an artist whose work I greatly admire. I'd like to take a little detour to better understand the connection, the echoes between Dempster's and Goodwin's works, and in so doing I'll be quoting from the catalogue, *The Art of Betty Goodwin,* published by the Art Gallery of Ontario at the time of a retrospective of her work that showed from November '98 to March '99.

In the introductory essay Anne Michaels writes that Betty Goodwin "annihilates metaphor." Goodwin's series of vests, many of them consisting of actual garments, while others are lovingly rendered in soft-ground etchings, represent the raw struggle of love trying to break free of loss. "How does love leave its mark?" Michaels asks. "Through memory, possessions, an imprint on flesh..." How does this annihilate metaphor, I ask?

Anne Michaels's essay is followed by another, written by the AGO's Director at the time, Matthew Teitelbaum. He writes that some of the vests "were remnants of her life, others gathered from vintage clothing stores and chosen for their lived-in qualities... The vest was the icon of her father-figure and art-mentor, Joseph Beuys, who often wore a vest during public appearances. Goodwin's works using articles of clothing, and the Vest Series in particular, share a deeply felt elegiac quality. They suggest that images can encapsulate states of remembering and communicate that quiet desperation inherent in the struggle to hold on to an idea or a feeling that is lost or soon to be lost."

Here's that word, *loss*, again. Does the fact that Goodwin uses and manipulates actual objects to convey, symbolically, the love of someone lost, mean that she annihilates metaphor? Does the fact that the speaker of *The Burning Alphabet* cherishes, above all, "the explicit," mean that he can get rid of ambiguity?

One more quote, from Betty Goodwin herself:

> I am trying to realize and express my personal vision of the world around me as vitally as possible. I want to use the elements of shapes, spatial relationships, rhythms, colour, to build a structure in which a meaningful content and the objects in the painting possess an intense reality, revealing more than the visible. I want to obtain the very essence of their being in relation to my idea.

What makes Goodwin's ideas so palpable are the various elements she uses—shapes, spatial relationships, rhythms, colour—in order to obtain the essence of their being in relation to her ideas. She's not saying that her work embodies truth, she is saying that her work, such as the Vest Series, stands in place of truth and embodies her *idea* of truth. There is a difference.

What does the speaker of Dempster's poems do when he believes the gods have abandoned him, or God is toying with him, or that the past, including his own, is disappearing? He sits down and "light[s] a fire in the first available emptiness"—the emptiness that Barthes and Benjamin write about in the quotes chosen by Dempster. What is Dempster's fire made of? It is made of language that sears, language that penetrates different layers, much as Goodwin's art does. In her series, "La mémoire du corps," her pastel and graphite drawings penetrate the mylar skin on which she explores her *idea* of bones and nerves. Instead of flowers in a vase, Dempster sets out, in writing, a display of a pet's bones, Clytie's tiny, white bones. What are Dempster's bones made of? Letters of his fiery and burning alphabet.

The back cover of *The Burning Alphabet* claims that "Underpinning Dempster's poems lies an unswerving dedication to emotional and spiritual honesty." In my search of reviews on Dempster's work, I encountered recurring claims describing his poetry as "honest" or words to that effect, such as, "Dempster's poetry is a *truthful* way of rendering consciousness," etc...

According to the old binary of opposites, these comments imply that if there is honest poetry there must be dishonest poetry. What is it, in some people's minds, that makes some poetry "honest," and other poetry "dishonest?" What is truthful consciousness versus untruthful consciousness? I wonder if it doesn't have to do with some readers' expectations being reinforced when those readers can't see beyond their expectations, thereby making, in their minds, the writing more honest, more truthful. It's very reassuring for readers to have their expectations validated, but it is also dangerous for writers or artists. When a writer is expected to contract forms of insurance in writing, the writing becomes a monument, what I call co-operative writing. It co-operates with what is expected of it. It brings a kind of death to the writer, death of the imagination, death of creativity, death as the closing out of the world. It is a self-annihilating immolation, different from the immolation that Dempster and Goodwin explore through their art forms, for theirs is a *mutated form of energy,* a phoenix rising from the ashes in the form of a handprint in a cave, in the form of Clytie's bones, in the form of vests in Betty Goodwin's art.

Dempster's words do not embody honesty or truth, they embody his *idea* of truth. What makes some art or some poetry better than others isn't necessarily whether it is representational or experimental or avant-garde, it is how well each artist or writer explores genre and form as the organizing principles for the embodiment of *ideas.*

Other people's deaths often put one's own into perspective. As another quote used by Dempster from Elias Canetti indicates, "Dead, one is not even alone any longer." Dempster's series "The Crowd of Him" is unusual in its blend of tenderness and pain, a blend of sorrow and anger, "Gunning my father poems, feels more slasher than son." These poems take the reader to the other side of nostalgia. Nostalgia, Dempster reminds us in "Mr. Memory," is compulsive, a sentimental longing for the past. Dempster's poetry is far more about the present moment of writing, of weighing each word, of struggling with the page as a potentially reactive space, than it is about nostalgia.

Dempster is best known as a lyrical poet, and I wondered at first if he wasn't also a writer from the Romantic school of poetry, when writers attempted to go beyond death by going through death, their encounter leading to an expansion of consciousness. Yet, the more I read Dempster, the more I had the feeling that the speaker of these poems kept moving towards what the poet John Ashbury has called the lyric crash. There is great conflict going back and forth between the explicit that the speaker of the first poem yearns for and his clear understanding that no matter how hard he tries to capture the autobiographical self it cannot be located in the imaging of a past. No matter how hard the writer tries to recapture his dead father, or even himself as he too faces illness, both remain, as the title of one poem suggests, "Missing Persons." It is on this conflict on which the poems balance so precariously that they often seem just short of the great fall anticipated by the poet, much as his father's tumble over a Persian carpet, or Goodwin's image of a figure falling on the cover. The "I" of these lyrical poems keeps crashing inside the gap between the lyrical "I" of the past and the "I" on the page who has to keep reinventing himself in poem after poem.

Wallace Stevens, another writer quoted in the first poem, "Explicit," is well-known for his phrase that writers live by "necessary fictions" and look for a new knowledge of reality. This implies that what we are presented with in literature is never the real thing—not a real heart, not the real person, not the real story. We are, instead, presented with bigger-than-life fictions necessary for the peeling back of different layers of understanding, for, in the end, we are all orphans in the country of our own creativity, our own thought.

To end, I would like to go back briefly to the first poem, "Explicit," where, coupled with a mention of the heart, there is mention of thought:

> Feel each finger as it creates
> a hand, each heartbeat billowing
> a Niagara of blood, each
> thought a circle so round
> it makes the moon look slack.

Heart and thought in this stanza can only be represented if they are given form. The line, "thought a circle so round," reminds me of the philosopher Karl Jaspers's line: "Being is round." What does this mean, I wonder?

Rilke wrote that once a thing becomes isolated, it assumes a figure of being that is concentrated upon itself; therefore it becomes round. Is this what Jaspers and Dempster meant? Not unlike the figure of the father who was isolated and concentrated upon himself until, in death, he became a crowd of figures inhabiting the poet's world?

Or does the speaker of the poem mean that the imagination of round thought follows its own law as each artist and writer must? If so, how big is this roundness? Is it as big and round as the world is round? Is it as big as the globe that the speaker of one of Dempster's poem carries under his arm?

The more I thought about this, the more the image of round thought became wonderfully complete in its own roundness and the more I found myself in the presence of an image outside explicit meaning. Heart and thought. Two invisible entities make their appearance at the heart of writing.

BOOKS CITED
Dempster, Barry. *The Burning Alphabet*. London, On: Brick Books, 2005.
The Art of Betty Goodwin. Bradley and Teitelbaum eds. Toronto: The Art Gallery of Ontario, 1998.

New Configurations for an Old Alphabet: The Art of Barbara Caruso

> We all lived in the spirit of a genesis.
> —*Theo van Doesburg*

ABCDEFGHIJKLM
NOPQRSTUVWXYZ

Van Doesburg's alphabet

Whenever I spoke with the artist Barbara Caruso, I was struck by the precision of her thought and the clarity of her language.

I experienced this for the first time in a telephone conversation, some time in the late seventies. I had seen collaborations she had done with the writer bpNichol, plus several drawings and a large canvas from her Colour Lock series in bp's house, and been so intrigued that I phoned her to ask if she would consider exhibiting in the art gallery where I worked at the time. I think I also asked if she would let this particular gallery represent her. Her response was polite but firm, something to the effect that she did not like the commercial aspect of galleries. I can't remember her exact words but I do remember the quiet conviction with which they were spoken.

I respected her decision, although I was puzzled by it. Had I been better acquainted then with the principles informing her and her art, I would have better understood the reasons behind her refusal. Caruso dispensed with the decorative and materialistic aspects prevalent in much of the art produced for and represented by large commercial galleries. Vague and hackneyed concepts of lyricism, symbolism and the subconscious were not part of her process. As much as she needed to sell her art in order to sustain the making of it, she was one of those rare artists who thought that the commercial marketing aspect of art could corrupt the end product. Nor did she seem concerned with individualism. It wasn't that she was self-effacing, but as she spoke her precision and enthusiasm always related to the work itself, giving the impression that it existed beyond herself. Her interest in Elementarism, for example, which stresses fundamental and elemental shapes that are universally recognized versus ones that are discretionary and arbitrary, had long influenced her. Ironically it also made her a rare individual in a world where so many artists conform to artistic expectations in their quest for individualism.

I also remember being in her home in Paris, Ontario, in the summer of 1988, lunching on omelet and salad. Few afternoons linger in one's mind for so many years. It was even more memorable since I had driven there from Toronto with bpNichol one month before he died. As I think back to that afternoon, bits and pieces of conversation resurface as if they had been waiting all those years to be remembered: "A painting of a cloud is not a painting of a cloud, it is about form and colour. Rather than concerning itself with subject matter, each painting and drawing should concern itself with form and colour within the four sides of a page or a frame," she had said. Or, as she has also written: "The size and shape of the page is the first decision. The activity takes place within. Even if a drawing suggests activity beyond the page, it is not there. It is on the page."

After lunch that day we spent a few hours viewing a series of drawings Caruso was working on while she patiently explained the thought process that went into each piece. I suspect she reiterated these explanations to different people for several reasons: she loved articulating the ideas that put into motion the lines of each drawing or the colour of each canvas. Caruso didn't leave much to chance. Each drawing or painting was completed in her head before it was committed to paper or canvas. Its production then revealed the technical perfection that equaled its concept.

I suspect there was another reason why Caruso so willingly spoke of her work: it was crucial that viewers understood it. She was concerned that each viewer got it right, or at least didn't get it entirely wrong. Because of this, I will quote directly from her program/invitation to her 2002 exhibition held at Artword Gallery in Toronto: THE ALPHABET PROJECT: PART 1:

> In 1981, I made *Van Doesburg's Alphabet*, a series of 26 drawings. Each drawing is a letter of the alphabet integrated with the square shape and the square page. I exhibited the drawings in 1982... In 2000, I turned again to this orthogonal alphabet and began a new open-ended series of drawings to explore and exhaust the potential I see in its square shapes and the rigour of its relationships.
>
> Theo van Doesburg designed his alphabet on the square using the horizontal and the vertical. The letters integrate perfectly with a square shape. In my drawings, I close the letters and draw the square shapes with lines in four directions: horizontal, vertical and two diagonals. I add ten square shapes (or more) to the 26 letter shapes, often making four of them read THEO, to acknowledge the author. The alphabet is Theo's but the drawings are mine. I make them out of my consciousness

of the order of the square and of the stacking and packing of the square shape on the square page. Each drawing is an individual work that visits (revisits) my history along with Theo's.

The exhibition area at Artword Gallery was long and narrow, each white wall broken by a doorway. Caruso's drawings were positioned at eye level on three walls, the distance between the 32 drawings calculated so that they ran along the left wall, across the back, and down the right wall, forming what could only be described as Van Doesburg's letter "n" (see illustration at top of essay). As I approached the first drawing, I recognized the smaller squares within the larger square of the frame. I keep one of Caruso's drawings of Van Doesburg's alphabet from her *Serial Works* exhibition of 1999 in my study where I can see it from my desk. I often look to its precision for inspiration.

Viewing Caruso's work always takes a few seconds to readjust one's optical references. Not only does it take a while for the eyes to adjust to the different shadings of grey and black against their backgrounds, it is crucial that enough time be spent to discern each one's particular configuration. "No drawing is the same," Caruso has said.

I had just begun viewing the drawings along the left wall when I overheard a man asking Caruso that old and tired question put to so many artist and writers: "Where do you get your inspiration?" To which Caruso replied, "Look at the drawings and you'll find out."

The four letters comprising the name THEO appear in almost every drawing. As Caruso pointed out in the program, in almost all of the drawings she added ten squares or more to the 26 letters of the alphabet, making four of them read THEO to acknowledge the artist/author who so sparked her curiosity and interest.

In order to better understand the extraordinary process of Caruso's drawings, it is important to briefly examine the principles behind Theo van Doesburg's art, including his alphabet, his writing, and the magazine *De Stijl*, which he edited from 1917 until his death in 1931. The first issue contained his introduction to an essay by Mondrian, "Neo-plasticism in Painting." Mondrian's first Neo-plastic paintings using rectangles date from that year and were the starting point for a series of pictures that moved away from naturalistic representation towards an abstract and plastic expression in which elements are transformed into a dynamic equilibrium. Van Doesburg referred to his work during this period as his elementary Stijl-period when he designed Neo-plastic stained-glass windows, tile floors, and colour schemes for buildings and houses.

"De Stijl" is Dutch for The Style—style as the integral relationship of the parts to the whole and of the whole to the parts. Accordingly, Van Doesburg created a design for the magazine that would express this concept. All the printing for *De Stijl*—including posters, manifestos, leaflets and the magazine itself—appeared in a new form. In the same way that Van Doesburg wanted to liberate colour and line from naturalistic representation in painting, he emphasized the autonomy of letters in typography. The letters could not, of course, be completely autonomous, since he wanted the magazine to be read, but he did want to stress the visual potential of the letter shapes and the arrangements of the text. He experimented with shapes of the alphabet as a visual means by which the total composition of the magazine became increasingly important. Blocks of text and letters could be placed horizontally or vertically. Red was used to stress certain graphic elements within the design, all in keeping with the principles of De Stijl. Some of these principles, to name but a few, were: orthogonality, geometric lines pertaining to right angles and rectangularity and the linear transformation of forms preserving length and angles; the use of pure colour, i.e., red, blue, yellow (think Mondrian) or black, grey and white (as in Caruso's Alphabet Project); the use of strong oppositions such as horizontal and vertical lines, but also diagonals; harmony and disharmony by means of oppositional planes and colours; concentration; suppression of predominantly individualistic and spontaneous approaches; mechanization, automatization and elementary construction. Van Doesburg's involvement in diverse art forms and styles reflects the De Stijl principle that artists should strive for harmony between disciplines. He, in fact, adopted different pseudonyms for different disciplines. He was born Christiaan Emil Küpper but adopted his stepfather's name, Theodore Doesburg, adding "van" when he decided to become an artist at the age of eighteen. He subsequently invented two more pseudonyms: a Dutch alter ego, I.K. Bonset, under which he published his Dadaist poems and essays; and an Italian pseudonym, Aldo Camini, under which he published philosophical treatises. He even managed to keep his use of pseudonyms undetected for a while, and there is a delightful story of Mondrian complaining to Van Doesburg that he thought the poet I.K. Bonset was trying to steal their ideas.

This is not to say that Caruso's drawings observe categorically—from A to Z, if you will—Van Doesburg's ideas. Her drawings are created in the spirit of the genesis that Van Doesburg referred to, genesis as an opening to new ideas, as a new beginning.

It is, of course, impossible to convey an impression of a drawing without the actual drawing, but Caruso refused to have any of hers reproduced for this essay, for fear the dynamics of the drawings would be lost through reduction to fit the small page and through the poor quality of a reproduction.

The drawings were, first and foremost "abstract paintings," Caruso insisted as she offered to guide me from drawing to drawing. They were also rigorously planar, with no curvature whatsoever, although the intersecting lines did create an effect that seemed to refute this at times. They were unquestionably intellectual inasmuch as they provoked thought and reflection. But what struck me most was their intimacy. To Van Doesburg, art meant intimacy, and what better way to create a feeling of intimacy, but to enclose.

As Caruso explained, Van Doesburg's design of each letter integrates perfectly with a square shape and she closed each letter in a square filled with horizontal, vertical and diagonal lines. Each square was energized by a motion of intersecting lines; the different, and surprisingly varied, patterns were achieved according to the sequence of the lines drawn and the various sizes of pen nibs used. Usually, in a painting using colour, the energy projected is determined by the colours and their relation to each other. In the Alphabet Project, the fundamental colours of black, grey and white, along with the vertical, horizontal and diagonal lines, were energized by their dynamic counter-compositions, or by their relation to each other. This resulted in a moiré effect of constant movement, not unlike an optical illusion that keeps readjusting the perception of the viewer.

From the first drawing, I wanted to discover how one differed from the other. Although the letters read serially from left to right, the seriality was sometimes interrupted in order to draw attention to a particular letter and to the relationship between letters. For example, in *Alphabet 3,* the letter A was made of only two verticals and two horizontals and it was not inked in as in most of the other squares. This emphasized the fundamental elements that go into the making of this particular alphabet and in Caruso's drawings. This was also the case in other drawings in which some of the squares do not contain letters, but two diagonal lines intersected inside a square forming an X. Again, these lines served to underline the elementary compositions of the drawing but also drew attention to the performative potential of each square space. Caruso did this over and over again throughout the series, drawing attention to the potential of the square within the square. It didn't take long to grasp, through these very simple lines, the source from which these drawings originated.

In drawings of earlier series, the letters were orderly, reading from left to right. In this recent series, however, there was a shift in the orderliness, where letters sometimes 'wandered' into the margins and the viewer's eyes were forced to follow. In others, the eyes moved fluidly because the sides of the square touched, creating maze-like spaces, while in others, a definite verticality had been created where the letters did not abut. In another, all the letters had been pushed to the edge of the paper so that there was little margin. In all of them, the light and dark lines that went into the making of each configuration required the eye to adjust in order to extract the negative/positive effects inside the squares, each square made, in a photographic sense, of both its negative and positive elements. In Caruso's own words:

> In each drawing, the letter shapes read serially left to right. That seriality is interrupted to bring emphasis to a particular letter (X), the relationship between two letters (S & Z), three C,N & U) or more (E, M, W, S & Z), and to the square shape drawn in one, two, three or four directions, or as a contour shape. The shapes on the square page configure to have a 'margin' commensurate with the shapes on the page. Having established the composition and explored it over and over again, I began drawing shapes in that margin until it was filled. The size of the drawings is uniform, 15" x 15". I work the whole page and frame accordingly.*

It is obvious that Caruso spent much time not only in the planning of each drawing but in its execution. Her technique was precise, the results sometimes simple, sometimes intricate, the configurations often surprising in spite of her reluctance to leave

---

* From Caruso's invitation/program to the exhibition.

little to chance, qualities she seemed to expect from others. I tentatively explained to her how I intended to proceed with the writing of this essay. "So you have a plan," she said as she nodded approvingly. "Keep it simple," she added.

There is a notion in certain critical and theoretical circles claiming that a work of art, whether it be a painting, poem, or novel, can only be completed when viewed or read or when it has undergone critical analysis. Caruso disagreed. "When I am finished with a work, it is complete," she has said, and added that it may complete something in the viewer, but as a work of art it stands on its own. This may be so, yet Caruso obviously attended to a need in herself when she decided to create a series from Van Doesburg's alphabet. In fact, next to Caruso's drawings, Van Doesburg's letters seem oddly incomplete. It is the relationship between his letters and the square in which they are enclosed that complete each of Caruso's configurations. Each drawing is synthesized within its own logical construction.

As Caruso guided me from one drawing to another, she commented that creating an alphabet on a square grid could make it difficult, if not impossible, to read. "But how beautiful it is to look at," she quickly added. As a visual artist, Caruso was responding to the optical or visual element, whereas my first concern was indeed the fluency with which the letters could be read, although I do agree with her that Van Doesburg's letters are beautiful to look at. Because of their configurations—thick vertical and horizontal lines—they are often impossible to read unless they are read within the context of the alphabet. For example, Van Doesburg's letter "X" looks more like an "H," and would not be recognized if it were not placed between "W" and "Y" (see above illustration). To a writer, the letter is the fundamental element of language, each letter relative to the other in the forming of words, each word relative to the next in the forging of meaning.

Acknowledging the latent energy of the letter as a basic component—the atom—of writing could, in fact, be compared to the principle put forward by Van Doesburg: the primacy of the straight line as a future means of expression.

As I walked away from Caruso's exhibition I felt a great deal of admiration for what I had just experienced. I felt grateful, and still do, that our paths crossed over a period of thirty years. As she indicated in her program, each one of her drawings is an individual work that visits and revisits history, hers and Theo's. Each time I see her work provides me with the opportunity to revisit part of my history along with hers: the first time I encountered her work; the first time I spoke to her over the telephone; an afternoon drive to her home with bpNichol, and another with my husband, Jerry; the time she and Nelson spent at my house immediately following bp's death. I am grateful for this sense of a personal history, details stored away that develop over time into the subjective constructs of my own memory and my own history. And yes, I admit to a trace of nostalgia, a word disdained by many. Why, I wonder, is it assumed that words and the ideas attached to them remain unchanging? Without glancing back there can never be objective or subjective constructs of history. As Foucault pointed out, the singularity of events should not be recorded within a monotonous and historical finality when they are, in fact, better rediscovered in the most unpromising, anonymous and unhistorical places. Perhaps in places and events as simple as a car ride on a warm summer afternoon, a simple lunch, a tour around an artist's studio, and art exhibitions that continue to challenge and inform.

The more I look at the Caruso drawings that I have acquired, especially the one by my writing desk, the more I become aware of the dynamism and harmony between the many elements at work in each: horizontal, vertical and diagonal lines; basic colours of black, grey and white; the positive and the negative; the interior and exterior of elemental forms; time and space; the past and the present.

And the future. I noticed as I got to the end of the exhibition that *Alphabet 32* did not include Theo's name, and I wondered what the next series would entail without his inspirational presence. What new genesis or beginning was Caruso planning in her search for a deeper understanding of what she had already explored for so many years? I did not dare speculate, since nothing in Caruso's art is ever speculative. But I can hardly wait to find out. In the meantime I give Caruso the last word:

> I began these drawings as an open-ended series, for I did not know how many works I would make to satisfy my curiosity about the potential of this subject. This exhibition is Part 1 of the Project; it includes *Alphabet 1 – 32*. The series is still open.**

WORKS CITED
Baljeu, Joost, *Theo van Doesburg*. London: Studio Vista, 1974.
Caruso, Barbara, *Wording the Silent Art*. Toronto: Mercury Press, 2001.
Haffe, H.L.C. , *De Stijl*. Cambridge: Belknap Press of Harvard UP, 1986
Overy, Paul, *De Stijl*. London: Studio Vista, 1969.
Foucault, Michel, *Language, Counter-memory, Practice*. Ithaca: Cornell UP, 1977.

I am grateful to Barbara Caruso for having suggested sources and for so generously discussing her work.
    An early version of "Barbara Caruso: New Configurations for an Old Alphabet" was published in *Open Letter*, Seventh Series, Number 7, Spring 2003. The present tense in this essay was changed to the past tense due to Barbara's death, December 30 2009.

As the two following letters indicate, Barbara and I sometimes wrote to each other. She knew of my interest in art and my visits to galleries and museums when I travelled and she requested that

** Invitation/program

I send her postcards and commentaries on what I'd seen on such visits.

The following are excerpts of two letters that I sent to her in 2009. I'd heard she wasn't feeling well, but had no idea how seriously ill she was. The second letter was sent two weeks before she passed away.

June 1, 2009
Toronto

Dear Barbara

No! Your letters are not boring! And you understood my essay on Dempster's poetry more than you give yourself credit. It seems, in hindsight, presumptuous of me to have sent it. Dempster's book was "assigned" to me by the organizer of the course who purposely paired poets with different styles and thematics.

As for the points you make in your letter, yes, some of my comments were meant to challenge both class and poet, especially his claim that he wants his poetry to be "concrete." The word "stone" is not the stone. The only aspect of poetry that is concrete is the language itself and not necessarily what it represents or describes. Language poets are often, as far as I'm concerned, as concrete as lyrical poets.

I'm surprised that you have problems around the notion of "the reader as writer." I've always thought this a given. Every reading rewrites the text according to the knowledge and perception brought to it. For example, the writer who delivered an essay on my book—*Site-Specific Poems*—for the Influency Salon suggested that I had been influenced by T.S. Eliot... whom I've barely read... The class thought, as I did, that he'd completely misunderstood my poetry, and although I am not generally hung up on an author's intent I do expect, within the context of a course, that a reader inform himself on the writer he's writing on. But he only brought his own knowledge of early twentieth-century English and American Literatures and, as such, "literally" rewrote my book in his own mind. Certainly not in mine.

Re: my "honesty/dishonesty" comment. Of course, it won't change the minds of those who use it as an excuse "to tear strips off artists," as you say, but I still insist on making the point. I believe more people should.

I don't know anything about Dempster's personal health, and I don't think this is important to an understanding of his book. To me, his dis/ease is an existential one, an unease with being in the world. It stems from a Romantic tradition and has been done to death and I too am somewhat bored by it. Except there was something more, or maybe less, to Dempster's book, what I call the "lyrical crash" because it did "literally" crash as a "concrete" effort, and I rather liked that aspect about it.

What is round, you ask? Well, Van Gogh wrote: "Life is probably round." Karl Jaspers wrote: "Every being seems in itself round." Jules Michelet thought that a bird was solid roundness. Rilke's trees propagated in green spheres, and he referred to the bird's cry as "the round bird-call." Malevich's black circle against white has been described as "iconic roundness." I assume that poets, philosophers, phenomenologists, associate the form of roundness with permanence of being.

We did have five wonderful weeks in Paris and I'm more than happy to tell you about some of it. We did much, so this letter might go on a bit, but remember you asked for it! We first went to **Jeu de Paume** which is now a venue for photographic exhibitions. There were two retrospectives, one by Robert Frank and the other by Sophie Ristelhueber. I know that R. Frank was supposed to be very innovative since he was one of the first to shoot ordinary street scenes with ordinary camera, etc... but I am not as taken with his work as many people. I find too many of his photos clichéd ideas of what America is/was. Or perhaps we have seen his types of photos so often now and they have become clichés after the fact. His photo of Jews in Florida titled "Miami," and those of Blacks and cars in Detroit, titled "Detroit," seem to fulfill expectations of what those cities are supposed to be about. The photo of umbrellas in the rain titled "Paris" was the final straw for me. I could almost hear accordions in the background.

Ristelhueber's photos, on the other hand, presented new ways of looking and seeing, undoubtedly because she is contemporary. Her overview shots of war in the desert, each one mounted on aluminum sheets about 4ft x 6ft, looked like abstract paintings emphasizing the abstraction of war for those who look at it from a distance. In another series, a photo of the back of a nude woman with fresh sutures along her spine was reminiscent of Man Ray's "violin woman." An interesting juxtaposition—woman as aesthetic object versus woman as war victim.

Musée d'Art Moderne at Trocadéro for a de Chirico 70-year retrospective, a strange evolution from classicism to surrealism, some constructivism and back to classicism. Very "painterly," enigmatic, but I walked away with no great need to delve further into his art. Especially the last years when he duplicated (cannibalized) his earlier work. Dozens of self-portraits (as gladiators, centaurs and horses) grated after a while. One portrait I did like was of Apollinaire, painting of a classic bust with dark glasses, myth of the blind poet who sees mainly from the interior. Somewhat hackneyed, but I liked the representation of poet as a classic construct. I had never seen de Chirico's sculptures before, many of which reminded me of Brancusi. I did find the one-hour film of an interview shortly before he died interesting. Thematically, his life didn't seem to relate to his painting. He was as simple a man in life as his art was complex, and his sharp sense of humour contradicts the metaphysical gloom throughout his work.

The Pinacotèque for a huge Utrillo and Valadon exhibition. I was not that keen on seeing Utrillo, but I was curious about his mother, Suzanne Valadon. I had never seen her work and it was a surprise. It's as vibrant as her son's is flat. Wonderful sense of colour. I did get the impression, however, that because she was entirely self-taught she borrowed heavily from artists she befriended and I detected in her paintings Cézanne's trees, Gauguin's native women, etc... And she befriended many artists of the time. She is the woman in at least three of Renoir's paintings—"Girl Braiding Her Hair," his famous "Dance at Bougiva," and a profile whose title I forget. She is also the woman in Lautrec's "The Hangover" and she posed for several Degas. Her portraits of her son are amazing. Overall more interesting than Utrillo whose paintings, when grouped together, confirmed my belief that he painted mostly from postcards to earn money for drink. Although, I must admit, there were a couple I would never have recognized as his and liked—flat, frontal views of buildings without those annoying street perspectives he's so famous for.

Musée Maillol. All of Maillol's sculptures of women look pretty much alike, which is not surprising considering so many are of his mistress Dina Vierny. Or perhaps he only saw women as a unified form. Vierny must have been an interesting woman in her own right since her private collection at the Maillol museum includes works by Matisse, Cézanne, Degas, Gauguin, etc... The more interesting rooms, however, housed a temporary exhibition of Russian cubo-futurists and constructivists, the private collection of George Costakis, a Greek artist who lived in Russia in the early part of the twentieth century. He was able to get his own paintings and his collection out of Russia after the communist takeover. Here I thought of you. There were works by Lissitzky, Gabo, Pevsner, Malevich, Rodtchenko, Klioune, Koch, even Van Doesburg! I wanted to buy postcards to send you, but there was such a line up at the cash register and only one person manning it that I gave up. Now I wish I hadn't.

Many more exhibitions that I could write on. Zadkine whose sculptures I don't care for, but there were a few drawings I liked because of their pen tracings—one of which I am enclosing on a postcard. Bonaparte in Egypt (Double Yawn). **Musée Nissim de Camondo** overlooking Parc Monceau, mansion of wealthy bankers who came to Paris in the nineteenth century. It houses a five-generation art collection. Exhilarating and disheartening since the last generation—two young adults—were sent to Auschwitz in 1942, ten years after de Camondo had willed the house and its entire art collection to France. France did nothing to protect the two young adults, but claimed the house and art collection nevertheless... **Quai d'Orsée** for a sculpture exhibition called "Forget Rodin," an evolution of sculptors from Lehmbruck, Maillol, Bourdelle, Brancusi... etc...

At the risk of going on much too long, I must mention the Calder retrospective at **Centre Pompidou.** Extraordinary. His famous mobiles were familiar but I was really taken by his earlier orthogonal geometric compositions, how he balanced stylistic alternatives of natural forms and geometry, the technical and the imaginary. He too used round shapes over and over, in mobiles and drawings, which an art critic referred to as "reduced models of the universe" with stellar gravitation. Returned to the Brancusi studio for perhaps the twentieth time since the 1970s.

There were several French movies, two on Marguerite Duras for whom I have great admiration; free concerts in various churches on Sunday afternoons. Church acoustics make great venues for eighteenth-century organs. Saw an exhibition tracing the evolution of jazz, with canvases by artists who were supposedly influenced by jazz, from Picasso to Basquiat, but I found this contrived. Considering the history of racism in France (at least vis-à-vis North Africans) and its fascination with the "exoticism" of black jazz musicians dating back to Josephine Baker, it all seems a strange paradox. There must have been four hundred people attending the exhibition the afternoon we were there and I didn't see one black person. Apparently, the exhibition had drawn more than 35,000 viewers by the time we attended and I wondered what percentage had been black.

Thank you for your generous offer, re: a painting we can both agree on as to price and size. Although price is always an issue, what has prevented me from getting a piece of yours larger than the ones I already have is size. I simply don't have the wall space. I love how those large expanses of colours add an extra dimension to the interaction between the colours you use but the only wall space that could accommodate such a piece, i.e. from the Colour Lock series, is the landing of the third floor where there's a guest room and where Jerry has his office. Except for Jerry and the occasional visitor no one would see it, including myself, since I seldom go up there. And one of these years, as age sets in, we are going to have to consider a smaller house or apartment. Another consideration: the third-floor landing is under a skylight and gets a great amount of sun. Would this affect the painting?

Do you foresee an exhibition in Toronto soon? I look forward to Volume III of your journals. Will it include events around Barrie's death?

I'm enclosing a few postcards and several photos taken by Jerry—designations on the back.

My best to you and Nelson.
Lola

December 3, 2009
Toronto

Hello Barbara

The last time you wrote, you asked if Jerry and I were going away for the summer and yes, we did spend several weeks in the Laurentians. We kept hearing reports that the weather in Toronto was terrible, but it only rained once in Lanaudière and, except for a couple of cool days, I went swimming every day. I'm not a very strong swimmer, so I navigated the small lake with flippers. No motor boats and nary a human except for our "kids" when they came to visit. We did see a bear, though. We had every intention of driving into Montreal to take in a few exhibitions, especially the Goodwin retro, but life was too peaceful and we never did make it. When I wasn't swimming, I buried myself in biographies, my favourite being Isaacson's recent bio of Einstein. All 600+ pages!

We did, however, spend time in New York in November. There were plays I wanted to see, as well as several exhibitions at Whitney, MoMA and Guggenheim. At the Whitney, I discovered the work of Roni Horn, which included drawings, photographic installations, sculptures and books. Her photographic installations are conceptually interesting in that they challenge perception. What seemed, at first, to be rows of identical photographs turned out to have been taken a few seconds apart and were not, in fact, the same. I particularly liked her installation of photographs of herself from childhood to young woman to older woman to man (not really, but very androgynous) which explores identity, gender, etc... The concept of unstable identity appeals to me, versus the inflexible characteristics that people insist on to define who they are and are usually false fronts. As interesting as Horn's work is, however, my heart is still firmly rooted in painting and drawing as visual art forms, undoubtedly a function of my age.

The Whitney also had a Georgia O'Keeffe retro—over 130 paintings, drawings, and sculptures, much of which I had seen at the G. O'Keeffe Museum in New Mexico several years ago. I do admire her work, but I also get a little bored with her large flowers and pastels. I prefer her geometrical lines of adobe houses with square "windows" and their wonderful relationships to southwestern colours. I did enjoy the room of photographs of her by Stieglitz, the voyeurism of it all...

I made a point of visiting the permanent Whitney collection—the huge Rothkos always blow me away; Stella, whom I admire; and de Kooning, who always leaves me with mixed feelings of admiration and aversion.

The next day was MoMA day. The mezzanine on the second floor has three large Frankenthalers which I loved. The two main exhibitions were a Bauhaus historical retro including many Klees, Kandinskys and other artists from the Blue Rider period; drawings, architectural and otherwise, by Gropius; works by several students of Kandinsky's, including Eugen Batz, etc... I spent a fair amount of time in these rooms until it was time to move to the other main retro, Tim Burton's. I only knew of him as a director of (fantasy?) films of which I'd seen only a couple, mainly because of my grandsons. I reluctantly dragged myself toward the first room whose entrance had been transformed into a gigantic mouth and I wondered how or if I was going to make it through a dozen or more rooms. The first corridor-like space displayed rows of comics/cartoons he'd done as a child and young man with recurring characters, and I was immediately reminded of bp and what he once said (or wrote?) about comics establishing their own mythic narrative of the imagination. Hmm... I thought, this could be interesting. As the rooms progressed toward Burton's more mature work—he was apparently influenced by German Expressionism—the viewer follows his evolution from comics to graphics to videos to films. The story boards and drawings for the films were exceptional, I suspect more so than the films themselves, although I might look for a few on video, except for the Batmans! In two filmed and extensive interviews, he never struck a false note when he talked about the different aspects of his art. No pretension, no games, all about the imagination, and his is prodigious. So I was happy to have seen it after all.

We kept the Kandinsky retrospective at the Guggenheim for last. It was fortuitous that we had seen the Bauhaus at Whitney a few days before since both exhibitions highlight Kandinsky's teaching days in Munich. The Guggenheim is the perfect place to display his large paintings. As I ascended the spiralling ramp, I was astounded by the impact of vibrant colours and arabesques. We were there for a few hours—I was reluctant to leave—until I looked down from the upper ramp and saw Jerry patiently waiting for me on a bench in the lobby. It was as glorious spiralling down as it had been going up. The side rooms with his works on paper were also remarkable, their details as precise as the large gestures of his oils are bold. I hadn't realized the extent of Schoenberg's influence. The two corresponded at a time when Schoenberg was breaking with tonality in his compositions, and Kandinsky was making the transition to abstraction. I am curious how you view Kandinsky since, unlike Van Doesburg's demand that "the forms of nature be eliminated and replaced by art forms such as lines, colors, and surfaces, Kandinsky sought a middle way between non-representation and a new definition of nature." This quote is from the exhibition catalogue.

Most evenings were filled with theatre since the primary reason for going to NYC was to see plays. I am thinking of adapting my novel, *The Other Sister,* to the stage, and wanted to "experience" this genre of which I know little, at least as a writer. Saw a couple of plays that were too "American Realism" for my taste, but also two of interest. *Nightingale* by actress Lynn Redgrave who wrote, directed and starred (solo) in a play about her grandmother. Not sentimental since the old gal was a difficult woman trapped in a hopeless marriage and didn't care much for her own children, especially her daughter, Redgrave's mother. While the material itself didn't prove to be all that exciting, and wasn't of much use to me, the backgrounds and changes of scenery were done by the projection of images onto screens. This gave me great ideas. Whether anyone else will think so is another matter... The other play I enjoyed was *The Understudy,* a delightful rendition of two supposedly famous Hollywood actors who are cast in Kafka's *The Trial*—but who understand nothing about it. The understudy thinks the director should introduce a gun scene and a dance number to make the play more palatable to a larger audience. A brave, intelligent and satirical send-up of Hollywood and the Broadway theatre scene.

So, there you go. Thought I'd bring you up to what I've been doing since I last wrote. Hope you and Nelson are doing well.

Do send news. Are you working? Have you visited the new AGO yet? I don't care for the small rooms on one of the upper floors but the Galleria Italia at the front with its emphasis on wood and tree forms is, I think, a perfect blend of engineering feat and aesthetic triumph.

Lots of peace and joy during the holiday season and a great 2010 to both!!!

Lola

On December 31, 2009, I received a message that Barbara Caruso had passed away the day before. I wished then that the last letter I had sent had been different, yet Barbara probably would not have wanted me to change it much. Her drawings in my study, in my living room, and the collaborations she did with bpNichol, also hanging in several rooms of my house, are constant reminders of her creativity and her fine spirit.

The Errors of Their Ways

> "Lack" does not reside in the ignorance of a language, but in the non-mastery of an appropriated language. The authoritarian and prestigious intervention of the French language only strengthens the processes of "lack."—Edouard Glissant, *Le Discours antillais*

It should be stated from the beginning that I have the utmost admiration for people who take the time and make the effort to learn a second or more languages. Although I was born into a Franco-Ontarian family, I don't count myself among those people since I was never aware that I was learning a second language. I grew up in a mainly English-speaking neighbourhood and was oblivious to the fact that I was gradually displacing my own French mother tongue. I have often felt envious of Francophiles who were more proficient in French than I was. Two such people who come to mind were the late Barbara Godard and the late Robert Dickson. It was fascinating to watch Barbara at conferences do simultaneous translations at mind-numbing speed. Robert Dickson, born into an English-speaking family, was a professor in the French Department at Laurentian University, taught and wrote in French, and won a Governor General's award for his poetry book, *Humains paysages en temps de paix relative*. I was fortunate and grateful for Dickson's translation of my first novel, *Frog Moon*, but it remains a source of regret that I wasn't able to write it in French. I tried. To write most of one's work in a second language for the sole reason that the first language has become deficient is tantamount to a psychological and physical wound that won't heal, not even into a scar.

Thanks, in great part to the Quiet Revolution and to the Québec sovereignty movement, it's been a while since Anglophones living in Montreal have dared tell a Francophone to speak "white" as in the Michèle Lalonde poem of the same name, written in the '60s; or, as in the '70s, when a waitress informed me that she wouldn't serve me unless I spoke English; or when I was told by a real estate agent in the early '80s that I wouldn't want to look for a house in Outremont surrounded by "pepsis." The epithet "pepsi" derives from the belief by some Québec Anglos that their French-speaking counterparts drank Pepsi because they couldn't afford the marginally more expensive Coke. It was also understood that the slur applied to those same French speakers because a bottle of Pepsi was empty from the neck up. The fact that it also applied to Coke or any other soda bottles didn't seem relevant. You can imagine the real estate agent's stupefaction when I informed her that I was, in fact, one of those "pepsis" and I would prefer to switch real estate agents. Once she recovered, she gave me the usual, sheepish response: "But you speak English so well."

I suppose I speak English well enough, although a few people have remarked that I sometimes speak it with a slight accent. I spoke French with my parents and still speak it with relatives, friends and acquaintances from Ontario, Québec, and France. Writing in French, however, is another matter. I become aphasic. Words and thoughts disappear. Doubt besets every sentence, every turn-of-phrase. What if I should make mistakes in my own mother tongue! I suddenly see myself cast in Michel Tremblay's *Les Belles-Soeurs,* trapped within a limited vocabulary, frustrated by my inability to express myself adequately in what should be my first language. Mind you, it also happens when I write in English, but not nearly as much. Robert Dickson related to me once that he had the same experience when asked to fill in for a colleague who taught Canadian Literature in English. He was so used to teaching in French that he too became aphasic before the English-speaking class. The words and ideas were simply not forthcoming.

A few decades ago it wasn't unusual for Anglos to tell a Franco-Ontarian that they understood and spoke French, but only the "Parisian kind." Does anyone remember that old canard? Supposedly, the French that Ontarians and Québécois speak is not only not up to standard; it is indecipherable to the finely tuned English ear. I am being sarcastic, but I still remember the authoritative and proprietary way in which this has been related to me more than once. At a neighbourhood party a few years ago, I overheard the host say that he had a wonderful handyman who had a delightful if peculiar way of expressing himself in Ontario French which, as we all knew, "is not really a language." And I wondered how we, linguistically deprived Franco-Ontarians, have ever managed to communicate anything.

If, as a young woman, I was too easily intimidated to confront a waitress, I have since grown impatient with a more insidious phenomenon. Strangely enough, it has to do with English-speaking people who proudly present themselves as "Francophiles." Several years ago, my pronunciation of the marketplace "Les Halles," enunciated without making the liaison between the "s" and the aspirated "h," was corrected by one of those Anglo Francophiles. No sooner had the two words been spoken than this self-proclaimed expert raised his eyebrows a few centimetres and corrected me with "Les (Z)alles," making the liaison as if the "h" was "muet." For those who do not know, or may have forgotten, when a French word begins with an aspirated "h" (as in "halles") it is treated as if the word began with a consonant and does not require the liaison. However, when a word begins with a mute "h" it is treated as if it began with a vowel and a liaison is required. I knew the right pronunciation yet the correction from my

Francophile friend was done with such authority that for a brief second I doubted myself. I felt the same way as when I had been told by a waitress to speak English if I wanted to be served. But only for a brief second. I overlooked his obvious scepticism. "Les Halles," I reassured him, was pronounced without the liaison, without the "z" sound.

A similar occasion happened when my pronunciation of the rue Malesherbes—this time pronounced with the "z" liaison—was corrected by another Francophile who regularly spends long periods in France. Again, this was conveyed with such authority that it sent me to the proper names section at the back of my Larousse: "MALESHERBES, [malzerb] Chrétien Guillaume de Lamoignon, magistrat et homme d'État français, etc." As if the dictionary wasn't sufficient proof, in the next few weeks whenever I took a taxi in Paris I asked the driver as to the correct pronunciation of *rue Malesherbes*, and each time, the answer came back: "Malzerb."

Twice I've been corrected on the name of Marguerite Duras, once by an Anglo Francophile, and once by a German. I pronounced the "s" at the end of "Duras" but was informed that I shouldn't. In which case, several interviewers on French television would be wrong. Bernard Pivot, the excellent commentator/interviewer of the two long-running programs, *Apostrophes* and *Bouillon de Culture,* favourite programs of mine while they lasted, interviewed Marguerite Duras several times and always pronounced the "s" at the end of "Duras." Duras herself is known to have requested that people pronounce the "s" in her surname.

Unfortunately, some Francophiles' authority is not relegated to spoken French only. Too often, when English-Canadian writers pen more than three words in French, one of them is bound to be wrong. I was very pleased to receive in the mail a copy of Stephen Scobie's *The Measure of Paris,* published by the University of Alberta Press. The book blends travelogue, memoir, literary criticism, poetry, and Scobie's personal observations to mark the time he has spent in Paris. In fact, Scobie's interest, appreciation and knowledge of the city have always impressed me. He was, as far as I was concerned, a true Francophile who relied, as he admits throughout his book, on his "expertise of the flâneur" when in Paris. I might as well admit up front that I have grown very wary of the concept of the modern-day flâneur still strolling leisurely through a wonderland of his construction. It might have worked for Baudelaire way back when but, since Walter Benjamin's use of the term in *The Arcades Project*, intended primarily as a nineteenth-century historical document, the concept has become a tired hundred-year-old cliché. Every tourist who now walks the streets of Paris and writes about it seems to think of himself as a flâneur, a peculiar guise given the arcades are now labyrinths filled with commercial goods where, on most days, it is unpleasantly difficult to walk through, let alone dally.

It was clear from the beginning of *Measure* that much of it revolved around the writing of expat writers who had spent time in Paris, and I looked forward to visiting various landmarks as experienced by these writers. It didn't take long to realize, however, that it wasn't necessarily other writers' experiences of Paris that I would be visiting. The measure mentioned in the title is mainly Scobie's, as he uses each writer's experience of Paris to frame his own. He is the standard by which other people's writing of the city is measured, in the true tradition of the flâneur.

For the most part, Scobie's book is anchored in a past gleaned from books and from what he calls "the persistent trope" about Paris. His geographical markers begin with boulevard Haussmann, named after Baron Georges-Eugène Haussmann, the well-known figure responsible for the Second Empire transformation of the city in the mid-1800s, considered to be the birth of modern Paris. Except for a few contemporary Canadians, Scobie's literary references are also mostly from the past: Glassco, Joyce,

Hemingway, Stein, Benjamin, Baudelaire, Proust, etc... All of which provide easy and comfortable associations, not unlike those explored in Woody Allen's film, *Midnight in Paris*, albeit Scobie's are more literary, theoretical and analytical. I must admit I was seduced, once again, by the opening shots of Paris skylines and famous landmarks in Allen's film, but I also recognized them as postcard shots intended mainly as clichés. It is also clear that only the very rich can afford to live in Woody Allen's Paris.

What I didn't find in Scobie's book is an impression of life in Paris today. He refers, in passing, to the traffic and bustle, to recent elections, exhibitions, films, but one never feels a present-day connection to the city. The face of Paris has changed considerably since Scobie first vacationed there. The city is besieged with ongoing strikes and demonstrations; the Americanization of everyday life with its chains of fast food establishments and supermarkets replacing family-owned shops; the relocation of the working class to housing projects in the suburbs; the generally poor quality of restaurant food except in exorbitantly expensive establishments, and so on. Scobie keeps reminding the reader—and perhaps himself—that he "keeps a cautious distance," that he is "a solitary man," that he is "detached from everything" around him, as a true flâneur would be. Faced with having to come to a realistic understanding of how Paris is now compared to how it was forty, or even two hundred years ago, he writes that he has decided to "take care of himself," which is all very well, but one is tempted to ask if taking care of one's self is the most important aspect of writing a book about another culture's city. He repeatedly reminds the reader that he is the observer which, in turn, also reminds the reader that Scobie is glaringly aware of his own observing. As such, his self-imposed image of the flâneur rarely manages to break through to the other side of his detachment, to any Other as differing from himself.

This short essay is not meant to be a critical review of the mournful and chronic nostalgia that permeates Scobie's book. Too many of us are guilty of the same transgressions when writing about Paris. What confused me however, given the book's authoritative tone, were the basic errors Scobie makes when he uses French. He doesn't, in fact, use much French, but the voice is so self-assured that when he does make errors they are all the more jarring. They are so basic. When he writes about a steak "cuit *au* point" and tells us that it is a steak cooked to perfection, he errs both grammatically and presumptively. It should be a steak "cuit *à* point" which is not, as Scobie states, a steak "perfectly done." A steak "cuit à point" is a medium-cooked steak. People who prefer their steaks either rare or well-done would not consider a steak "cuit à point" perfectly cooked. It is a passing mistake that could be quickly forgotten if he hadn't chosen to do an entire riff, a play-on-words on it, all based on an error. Other examples are his use of articles, "le" when it should be "la" or vice versa, as "*le* plage" which should be "*la* plage" or "*La* Zénith" which should be "*Le* Zénith." "Muguet *du* bois" should be "muguet *des* bois," and so on. I remember reading somewhere that if a writer didn't get articles and conjunctions right when speaking or writing in a language that was not primarily his own, it deprived nouns of their true voice. I couldn't agree more.

Other errors perpetrated due to Scobie's fondness of play-on-words are his use of "Jour née" which should be "jour né" if the two words are separated. This, of course, would destroy his riff on "journée" as a newly born day. He doesn't make any distinction between certain words, such as "le baiser" which means "the kiss," and "la baise," which means—there's no other word to use here—"fuck." According to Scobie, these two words are interchangeable and create ambiguity. In fact, these two words are not interchangeable and the ambiguity is entirely of his making. It saddles the novel he is discussing with an unfounded interpretation, again based on an error.

There are more examples, but I think I've made, even

overstated, my point. I once read that Paris was the capital of illusionism. Perhaps, for some writers, basic definitions and grammatical rules don't play a very important role in their detached world of illusions.

I recently received from the poet and food critic, Gerry Shikatani, an invitation to contribute to a series he was planning on food: *Les délices du table*. While I was flattered to be invited, why, I asked, would he give a French name to his series, especially given the fact that it was grammatically incorrect? It should be *Les délices de la table*. But more importantly, why use a French title at all? Would it be a French series on French food? I presumed not. Was it to give his series more cachet? How could it if the title itself was grammatically wrong? Was it another case of exploiting a stereotype? It reminded me of a point Jacques Derrida makes in *Sovereignties in Question: The Poetics of Paul Celan*, in which he points out that when adopting the gestures of another culture when speaking its language, one should be wary of adopting gestures that conform to stereotypes which homogenize the model of a supposedly "average" person from that culture. It gives the impression that the speaker is not telling the truth.

I've recently read Shikatani's collection of poems, *The Port's Seasonal Rental*, whose setting is a cottage on Lake Erie, published by Mercury Press & Teksteditions. Many of the poems in English are lovely, but scattered throughout the collection are thirty very short French poems. Admirable, an English reader might say, but not entirely so to a French reader. There are in these thirty brief poems as many errors or more, basic mistakes I'm not going to list because I find this kind of cavalier attitude towards language disheartening. In his acknowledgements, Shikatani thanks an Acadian writer for "his faultlessly perceptive work as editor" of his French compositions, a perplexing acknowledgement given the number of errors I suspect are not merely typos. I can only guess that either this editor didn't bother editing the French poems, or that the poems were printed from an unedited copy. In either case, Shikatani did not have enough command of the French language to avoid or notice the errors himself.

The fact is, neither Scobie or Shikatani gives the impression of *inhabiting* the French language, at least in their writing.

Many successful writers have chosen to write in a second language. Many have claimed that doing so has given them fresh perspectives on a language and culture that were not primarily theirs. I believe this to be true. The books mentioned here were written by English-speaking Francophiles, mainly for English readers who may not be aware of the inaccuracies. For those who do notice, however, the errors undermine the work of two writers whose books deserve better.

Speakers rarely wish to be misunderstood and writers rarely wish to be undermined. If only for CanLit's sake, and for the sake of a supposedly bilingual country, writers and publishers who are not fully bilingual and who insist on writing and publishing in a language that is not their own should make sure they get proper editing from qualified editors. Otherwise, they should limit themselves to their own language or, at the very least, learn to be a little less authoritative about someone else's.

WORKS CITED
Derrida, Jacques. *Monolingualism of the Other; or, The Prosthesis of Origin.* Trans. Patrick Mensah. Stanford: Standford UP, 1998.
Glissant, Edouard. *Le Discours antillais.* Paris: Gallimard, 1997.
Scobie, Stephen. *The Measure of Paris.* Edmonton: University of Alberta Press, 2010.
Shikatani, Gerry. *The Port's Seasonal Rental.* Toronto: The Mercury Press/Teksteditions, 2011.

Paule Thévenin

Paule Thévenin lived in Paris, France. For at least forty-seven years of her life she edited some thirty volumes of Antonin Artaud's *Oeuvres complètes,* published by one of France's pre-eminent publishing houses, Gallimard. She also edited Artaud's letters, *Lettres à Génica Athanasiou,* published by Gallimard in 1969. Over the years she wrote several pieces on Artaud's work for various literary magazines. These were assembled in one volume, *Antonin Artaud, ce Désespéré qui vous parle,* published by Seuil in 1993. It included the original version of "Lettre à un ami," which first appeared in the Belgian literary magazine, *Centre international d'études poétiques* in 1986.

I first came across this letter during a Paris visit, when friends who are admirers of Artaud and Thévenin gave me a copy. As soon as I read it, I resolved to translate it. I obtained Thévenin's address, we exchanged a few letters and she gave me permission to do a translation. The question of money came up and I pointed out (perhaps too curtly) that it was unlikely I would get paid much, if anything, for publishing a translation of a French document in a Canadian literary magazine, but that I would gladly pay her myself for her remarkable document. I felt somewhat abashed when I received her most gracious and understanding response. As it turned out, shortly after my translation appeared in *Canadian Fiction Magazine,* the magazine reimbursed me fully for the amount I had sent Thévenin.

In the spring of 1993, I received a copy of Thévenin's *Antonin Artaud, ce Désespéré qui vous parle,* published by Seuil. The back cover describes it as "a book that gathers Paule Thévenin's writings on Antonin Artaud: prefaces, commentaries on texts, clarifications, genealogical research, interviews, and anecdotal stories. This ongoing work and essays, an exercise in esthetic faithfulness and proverbial admiration, have graced the editing of *Oeuvres complètes* as both witness and a ray of light" (my translation). Accordingly, each chapter relates to a particular theme, from genealogical and biographical sketches, to music, art, and the theatre all of which played essential roles in Artaud's work. One of my favourite chapters, "Entendre/Voir/Lire" challenges the role of psycho-analysis in the study of literary texts:

> It would be important, once and for all, to stop reading Antonin Artaud's texts by the light of psycho-pathology. Any reading done in this manner is doomed to failure from the beginning.
> ... It can't be said loudly or often enough: all reading done at the feet of schizophrenia, all psychological or psychoanalytical explication of Antonin Artaud's work, every study of a text based on a classical connection to the mother or the father, all precedence given to organic or mental illness, cannot be used to deepen... a reading... On the contrary, [such readings] are but occult undertakings, masks thrown over the texts in order to disfigure them. *(my translation)*

The original French version of "Lettre à un ami" was also included in the book, and under "Origine des textes" I discovered that Thévenin had included my name as the translator of this letter, an unnecessary acknowledgement since the book did not include my translation. It was another indication of her generosity, a generosity I found admirable but not without frustration as I learned more about her lifelong devotion to Artaud's work. Anyone who has read Artaud is aware of his distrust of women, which can only be described, in spite of Thévenin's caveat cited above, as the deep-seated misogyny of a traumatized if inspired mind. To her credit, she was able to transcend one perspective in order to better understand the other, at least as much as this is possible. A few months after receiving the copy of her book, I learned that Paule Thévenin had died of throat cancer on September 25, 1993, at the age of seventy-five.

Letter to a Friend:
Paule Thévenin on Antonin Artaud

Paris, January 2, 1986
My dear Bernard,

Frans De Haes has asked me for an outline of my experience around the *Oeuvres complètes* of Antonin Artaud for the *Centre international d'études poétiques*. Since you know me so well you can imagine how this request embarrasses me, how unfavourably I look upon the personal and upon outpourings of the heart. To speak of this work, which is far from being completed, but which has been the thread of my life for forty years, is in fact to speak of myself. However, if his request embarrasses me, it nevertheless awakens in me the desire to respond, since I have never ceased to question myself on the profound meaning of living with this work—its continuance, its duration, the way my life has been marked by a task I decided I must see through when I was still very young. If this desire has been obsessive, it has not been so violent as to break the chains of my inhibition. It has, instead, gradually taken the form of a law to which I have consented.

Dogged by Frans De Haes's request, I find myself trying to define the problem posed by the writing of this letter. Why this letter, and why am I addressing it to you? It's very simple really. It came naturally when I remembered one of the first times we met. You had brought me a few letters of Antonin Artaud's and we spoke for a long time. The questions you asked about my work, the way you asked them, your attentive silences, the impression that at last I was being listened to, all made me tell you more in a few minutes than I had told anyone before. And all the while you conveyed the impression that not only was I not shamefully exposing myself but that I was revealing a truth sought by both you and I. In writing to you now, I am continuing an unfinished conversation. A few days after our first exchange, you said you'd been left with the impression of having assisted in something close to a primal scene. This troubled me, and troubles me still as I attempt to return to a subject around which I must once more circumvent my aversions, this time not only without the help of a friendly presence, but with only the souvenirs of past selves on which I must depend, and the unpleasant perspective of the white page that I must confront.

It all began with my first meeting with Antonin Artaud. I still see him in my mind sometimes, standing and writing in a scribbler against the mantelpiece. It was a sunny day. Why did an act as innocent and simple as that change the course of my existence so drastically?

The answer of course lies above all in what and who he was. This man, eating and offering me roasted peanuts without interrupting his writing, uttered phrases that were sublimely strange. Antonin Artaud did not speak differently from how he wrote. This is so accurate that the phrases he spoke on that day, which so profoundly struck me that I have never forgotten them, resurfaced in one of the scribblers that I deciphered and which will appear in tome XXII.

I sat and listened. I didn't know it then, but from this moment I was struck by his words which had the power to open secrets he alone could pierce and offer as evidence. He was fully aware of this particular knowledge due partially to the terrible experience he had just lived, but also because of the unrelenting exploration of his thought and body he had to assume in order to survive. One day, much later, when I protested his gashing a table with a knife, he was somewhat abusive because I had not grasped that each of those notches represented the trace of a struggle and victory against the many enemies assailing us daily. "I shouldn't begrudge you for not understanding what took me nine years of asylum to comprehend," he said.

During that month of June, 1946, I was completely free. After two years of internship in a psychiatric hospital, I had come to the brutal decision that I would give up medicine and hadn't even bothered to fulfill the last formalities: the clinical work and the thesis. I had thought, rather vaguely, of acting as a career, but soon abandoned it after auditing a few courses with Jean Vilar, mostly hiding behind crates in the basement of the Drouin Gallery. Too shy or too proud, who knows. In any case, simply feeding answers or reciting monologues did not correspond to what I had hoped for.

I must admit that the irruption that Antonin Artaud caused in my life did not surprise me. In looking back, the event seems as natural as it was inevitable. I found myself in the presence of a man who revealed to me a world alive with unexplored realities far from the banal work in which we vegetate, a universe that had been his alone and for whom the merest lapse of time brimmed with fullness, and the merest gesture was laden with meaning. All of which didn't prevent him from being kind, exquisitely courteous, as well as knowing how to laugh and make others laugh.

You know the rest; there's hardly any need to dwell on it. Not two months had passed when he asked me to transcribe the poems that were to make up *Artaud le Mômo*. I had never used a typewriter and borrowed one from a friend. All those poems were typed with two fingers. When, from time to time, I return to those old transcripts, I realize what patience Artaud must have had when he was complimenting my work. From then on, he dictated the texts he intended to publish. As I've often stressed, it was a method he favoured. Dictation allowed him to control the sonorous effect, modify the arrangements of syllables if the tone was not exactly what he was looking for, eliminate passages he thought unnecessary, or develop others. I have previously referred to this method as vocal writing. I can't think of a better term.

I have forgotten faces, names of people I once knew well, but I remember in detail the afternoon he dictated *La culture indienne* and *Ci-gît*. We are at the Bar Vert. I see the layout clearly; Bernard Lucas stands behind the bar, and we are working at the table near the door so we can take advantage of the faint light of that November day in 1946. Artaud sits on a chair in front of me. He is wearing his old black coat. I hear every inflection of his voice. We have come to a passage entitled "Commentaire." He dictates the numbered list of the *saligauds*—[wrongdoers, offenders]: *1 omlet cadran / 2 palaoulette tiran / 3 largaloulette vitran* (…). He relates how each term of the list also contains a graphic representation. As soon as he articulates one of them, spelling it if he detects the slightest hesitation on my part, he stops, leans over the large scribbler in which I am transcribing, and traces with a pencil the corresponding sign. An extraordinary apprenticeship if it can defy to such an extent the passage of time. I was far from suspecting then how these sessions with Antonin Artaud were fashioning me, how he was introducing me to the internal scansion, teaching me a process of reading that doesn't depend solely on the eye or ear.

To tell you that I didn't rebel sometimes against this influence, which can be brutal for a young person, would be a lie. More than once Antonin Artaud referred to that small army of the faithful few ready to follow him wherever he went, willing to help found the *Théâtre de la cruauté*. He didn't mean this only as a metaphor, since a network of stable friendships was essential to him, especially when he denounced the harmfulness of sex, declaring that all sexual acts could only add to his existing pain. How could I, without being immodest, explain that my thinking was not so far from his and that I acknowledged the denial upon which he insisted? In declaring the denial of my own sexuality, I could only affirm it. Condemned to silence, what a strange game was being played. A test was being imposed from which I couldn't escape. I found a makeshift solution by running away. A friend suggested temporary work in Morocco for an agency dealing with the Ministry of Youth and Sports. My memory here is not clear. I left.

Antonin Artaud wrote for me to come back so I could see what he had done of my portrait; he claimed he had surrounded it with phrases and objects. I came back. I read the words circling my face. He had written, inscribed, that I was his daughter appointed to be a faithful sentinel, adding that Ophelia had risen late.

It was pronounced; it was written and definite. In writing that I was faithful, he made me faithful. He forgave me, cancelled my mistake and the brief moment when I had been unfaithful. I could never, would never again, fail him like Ophelia.

Am I to believe he already knew the fate he intended for me in May 1947?

One afternoon the following fall, when he invited me to Ruc to eat a particular kind of cake, I told him I needed to find regular work and that it was impossible for me to remain forever on holidays. He thought about it for a few minutes and answered: "Don't worry, you can count on me. I will find you work."

As I've said, Antonin Artaud liked to joke around, but he wouldn't have done so when it came to such matters. His answer held promise, it asked me to have confidence in him, and as such it's impossible to see it only as a whim. Could it not serve instead as a sign, an additional sign that from that moment he knew, he foresaw my future and anticipated the work required for deciphering and publishing the pile of scribblers he would leave me? He subsequently wasted little time in bringing the manuscripts to the house for me to look after, so they would be secure, he said.

If I conceded that perhaps I was the one chosen to safeguard this trust, I nevertheless continue to ask myself: why me? Why not Colette or Marthe who were better qualified to undertake the responsibility of a publication? Did Antonin Artaud think Colette, whose portrait he dated May 22, 1947, two days before signing mine, in which she resembles Ophelia with long pale hair and lacquered eyes, too fragile? Did he think Marthe too obsessed with Kafka? He had indicated his annoyance around this more than once, as he had done in his long letter on the Cabala. Why, of the three, did he choose the rebel, the one who resisted him the most, the one who sometimes opposed him and never openly agreed with him? I don't know. I have no answer.

On March 14, 1948, Antonin Artaud died. I have already related how, the day before, he came to have lunch with us. Before returning to Ivry, he had suddenly decided to grant me the power that would allow me to publish his books. Where he normally didn't concern himself with legalities, this living example of defiance of the Law, the cast-off of society, wanted this power to have all the attributes, the guarantees of an official document. He insisted there and then that my brother go and purchase a stamped sheet of paper. My brother didn't find one at the post office which may have been closed that day. [Artaud] then found a thick sheet of paper on which he thought it sufficient to affix stamps and have them cancelled by the office of the mayor or such. I must admit that at the time Antonin Artaud's decision surprised me. I didn't see the need of such a formality just so I could continue to serve as an intermediary between him and his editors. Jean Paulhan and K éditeur were aware of the work I was doing for Antonin Artaud. They had grown used to me bearing manuscripts or corrected proofs or collecting money owed him.

The next day Antonin Artaud died and the full meaning of his gesture became obvious. The sheet of paper he had wanted stamped took on an emotionally symbolic significance far beyond the legality of one drawn by some notary. It was his last sign, the last message to me from Antonin Artaud. Those lines written in green ink became the tangible mark of what he had wished on the last day of his life. That paper told me that he was entrusting me with the fate of his last books, something he valued beyond physical life, especially *Suppôts et Supplications* which he considered the sum of all his writings, and whose delays in publication had disappointed him so much.

I didn't know it then—knowing and not knowing—doesn't everything happen in a narrow margin where we simply don't know that we are on the verge of knowing until at last we think we do know? Believing in what time has taught us, we find ourselves, in fact, only in a new state of ignorance, an ignorance that is applicable to something else. I didn't know then that I was leaving a man I loved very much, leaving his lively presence, the sparkle of his blue eyes, his sharp and extraordinary gaze, the variations of his voice, the way he carried his head, his hair thrown back, his way of standing and walking, the blended scent of laudanum and tobacco that emanated from him, the pressure of his hand, the strength of each finger, his stance a trifle formal when he stood on the doorstep before coming in. I was leaving the poems read out loud as soon as they were written, the funny stories, the fury and the invectives, all the legendary stirrings. I was leaving all this only to find the indestructible core of a life he wished to preserve. I didn't know then that I would be dominated, bewitched by these countless written words and that it would take me more time to read, transcribe, re-transcribe, see to the publication of hundreds of scribblers, than it took him to write them. I didn't know then that I would find him again, but differently. This man who left me in the presence of a being of which I only had an inkling was also Antonin Artaud and for me to get to know all of him would take as long as my life.

During the spring of 1948 it wasn't without naivety that I resolved to continue on my own the work to which he had prepared me in dictating all those pages, in insisting I recopy them before mailing them, letters whose contents he wanted to save, and leaving me to decipher those many scribblers. Roger Blin, who was so close and so affectionately devoted to Antonin Artaud, convinced me he had designated me for the task. He added that he would help me.

As I've already told you, Antonin Artaud had wanted to safeguard his manuscripts. He had borrowed an old chest from us in which he had stuffed, pell-mell, scribblers, letters and a few typed copies, keeping with him only those scribblers on which he was working. As soon as he finished one, he brought it to the house in a battered suitcase that had travelled to Mexico and Ireland and it was placed into the chest.

The chest remained closed until several weeks after his death. When I opened it I discovered, in a corner, amidst the papers, a large dead rat. It must have lodged itself in there at Ivry just before Antonin Artaud closed the lid to bring the chest to our house. Fortunately, the damage was minimal: the rat had chewed a few typed pages of *Cenci* and the borders of letters Antonin Artaud had gathered for *Suppôts et supplications*. A few words had been eaten, but copies had already been made and the damage was not irreparable. I told myself that this rat was the last enemy whose negative presence Antonin Artaud had felt and that it had been defeated. Chocked by the papers, the rat had been killed by what it had sought to destroy. When I told this story to Adamov, at the time when he was writing *L'invasion* and kept questioning me about the scribblers, he had also been struck by the incident and thought as I did that the death of the rat held a hidden meaning. To me it meant the endurance of what I had been entrusted by Antonin Artaud—the true symbol of his staying power.

It soon became apparent that the mere presence of this assignment was transforming me. Suddenly responsible for all those little scribblers, all those firebrands, I became aware that I would have to gather all my strength in order to defend them. I knew I would become a target exposed to the temper of a family undoubtedly unleashed because, perhaps subconsciously, it felt itself the symbol of a society against which Antonin Artaud had never stopped proclaiming his revolt, a revolt that the family itself prolonged.

I also had to take into account my daily existence. My husband was a gynecologist. A most wonderful friend, he insisted on releasing me from all material worries. It was his way of being part of the adventure. From then on my life is organized quite simply: I assume the secretarial work of the medical office which requires my presence at home, but which also leaves me considerable free time to decipher and type the scribblers. Awed by what I read, I work feverishly without a system—which I will acquire later through necessity—taking the scribblers as they come. Far from thinking that one day I will have to organize the texts with a more critical eye I transcribe without restriction or second thought. The result is the accumulation of poor copies stapled to each scribbler and placed on the shelf of the sideboard. This disorganized approach permits me, however, to realize the extent of the work of Antonin Artaud and to discover beauty and brilliance I had not suspected. I recognize that it is unthinkable that I keep this to myself and that I will have to publish all of it, but I don't immediately address the issue. It isn't long, however, before I recognize that I will have to do so and that the labour ahead will have to be precise.

Because *Van Gogh le suicidé de la société* had sold relatively well, albeit to a limited public, K éditeur did not hesitate to accept the contract for *Suppôts et supplications* when Louis Broder denounced it. The managing director, Simone Lamblin, had quickly perceived anomalies and gaps in the typed manuscript submitted to her. During the last months of Antonin Artaud's life she had given me incomplete pages to be corrected by him, notably the pages from *Interjections* for which he had dictated important changes. The manuscript, however, needed additional revisions and K éditeur gave me the task. I will not bore you with the details of what I was expected to do, the comparisons I had to make between diverse documents, relying strictly on my ear for passages which had been dictated, so that the corresponding manuscripts did not exist. I have disclosed all of this in my notes of the double volume XIV, when, at last, *Suppôts et Supplications* finally appeared. What I haven't said was how, before the publication itself, I revised the work again and again, four or five times at least, retyping the manuscript from the first to the last line each time, rewriting the notes because the first ones were so awkward. What I haven't said is how I worked this text to such an extent that I believe I know it, as we say, to the tips of my fingers... And it is not only a metaphor if one thinks of the thousands of times my fingers touched the keys of my old typewriter to transcribe each word. What my notes don't mention is the preparation required for organizing the texts, the original documents almost doubled by the additional pages on which I note disconnections between passages, the solutions arrived at and the reasons that motivated them. If I had included in its entirety the process of my work, the two tomes of *Suppôts et Supplications* would have been twice as thick. I only told the essential. Today still I have not stopped working on this text. As soon as I encounter an element I didn't know at the time of publication, an additional detail, I make a note on the page or on a square of paper which I insert in my copy of the book. All my copies of *Oeuvres complètes* are terribly scribbled, filled with notes and observations that carry the mark of an uninterrupted labour.

At the same time as K éditeur called on me, Gaston Gallimard asked to see me. He was a charming man who must have loved taking risks. It seemed a real challenge on his part to have entrusted the fate of *Oeuvres complètes* to a neophyte without a university degree such as myself. That I succeeded in the first test doesn't explain everything: my method of transcribing Antonin Artaud's writing allowed me to easily restore words and sections of sentences deemed unreadable and left blank in the galley proofs of the first volume that the printers had sent.

For these *Oeuvres complètes*, which no one would have guessed would eventually fill a library shelf, Antonin Artaud had himself drawn up a concise plan of four volumes which included only, it is true, the four titles published before his incarceration, but which nevertheless foresaw *new work added to each volume*. All this, however, was rather vague. Shortly after the death of Antonin Artaud, Henri Pariso proposed another plan to Gaston Gallimard, a four-part anthology.

I had another project in mind. Since a contract existed for *Oeuvres complètes*, even if that notion was not based on anything definite and, in any case, applied poorly to the textual material of Antonin Artaud, I thought it nevertheless presented a possible opportunity for the posthumous publication of all his writing. I discussed this openly with Gaston Gallimard. His answer was quick and clear. He assured me of his support and delayed the publication of the first volume to allow me to research lost texts in periodicals that were more or less unavailable. All this led to another discipline: research in libraries. It was very archaic then: no photocopying machines at the disposition of readers and everything had to be copied by hand. No field was thoroughly explored. No organized catalogue of periodicals as there exists today at the Doucet Foundation. One had to locate, by one's self, each periodical, issue by issue. It is perhaps unnecessary to have gone over all this, but I thought you might appreciate how, from this private process—deciphering for the pleasure, the joy of discovery—I then passed on to another stage where I had to take into account the anonymous but fickle group known as "the public." I wasn't sure how to edit a work, how to represent it, how to clarify it if need be. Because of my passion for Baudelaire and my deep admiration for Jacques Crépet who taught me so much, my gratitude toward him doubled. He became my model. I read and reread the editions he had annotated in order to understand how he proceeded and how he came to marry love and science so well. As I told you, I was naive. I believe I still am.

I'll skip over the various difficulties I encountered, the legal action against me by a family whom Antonin Artaud had never for one instant acknowledged had any rights over him or, for that matter, over what he had written, a family whom, he felt, censored him, a family of whom he had definitely refused to be a member; I'll skip over the years lost when the publication of *Oeuvres complètes* was so frustratingly delayed by unnecessary troublesome interference. All this is too well known for me to go over it again. I only want to express to you how pleased I am now at having been so utterly stubborn and never having given in to the pressure and the intimidation.

After an interruption of almost eight years, Gallimard Publishers called on me once more. Unable to overcome the opposition from the *rightful claimants* (what terminology, really) who obstinately refused to entrust the preparation of *Oeuvres complètes* to a female *créature*, (a name which, with all its nineteenth-century moralistic, petit-bourgeois connotations, I was to be called during the course of one of the trials) it was thought best to bypass the whole issue. I would do the work but remain anonymous. I almost believe now that this anonymity, to which I consented without any hesitation, was, in the final analysis, beneficial inasmuch as it afforded me immense freedom and saved me from paralysis.

I used those eight years with determination because I knew it would not be in vain. I searched for letters and old texts, deciphered systematically all the scribblers, learned how to classify them chronologically in files, labelled them for clarity, discovered the extraordinary essence of those written at Rodez. I knew the day I succeeded in typing all those scribblers, a small part of my work would be accomplished. The first year, Rober Blin helped me, the two of us spending long hours checking my copies. Subsequently, because of his theatrical work as a director, he no longer had the time for those sessions when we challenged each other's readings, but he felt he could let me continue alone without any risk since the momentum was established.

Little by little I work out a method. It's quite simple: I consider the work on a scribbler completed only if I believe I cannot improve my reading, only if I see no possible revision of the last reading I've done.

I believe I told you how I proceeded. When typing a scribbler a first time, I keep the breath lines in mind, as Antonin Artaud did when he dictated, so I can determine, for example, a new paragraph or the emphasis of a word in the middle of a line. To reproduce the manuscript line by line doesn't make sense. More than once, I noticed that even if some of the layouts seem to enliven the text, some are gratuitous. Also, if, according to the format of the page used by Antonin Artaud, the printed line could correspond either to one line, or to two lines. His writing spreads out widely on the page and one line will evidently hold fewer words if the page he has chosen is narrow. I find it necessary to link the visual with the ear. In trying to hear the text as Antonin recited it, in making it submit to a rhythmic test, it's possible to determine the natural pause that should be observed.

This kind of listening seems to me indispensable since he insisted that his texts were written to be spoken and heard. By paying attention to the inner cadence the reader of Antonin Artaud will be assured that I did not read him incorrectly.

I let the first draft sit, much as we let bread dough sit. I return to the scribbler a few months later, long enough to have forgotten my first reading although it hasn't stopped simmering in my head. I recopy it as if I had never seen it. I compare the two drafts; examine any differences between the two. I should add that while typing I more or less x-ray the text. I unravel what has been written over other words, analyze it, try to detect the initial letter traced, what word was underneath, decipher words, parts of phrases, crossed-out sections, and play, if necessary, with the light on the page, or if required, use a magnifying glass. What is hidden under what has been crossed out sometimes helps me to better understand the version he decided upon, especially when Antonin Artaud's handwriting is too hasty. I must admit the greatest problem is how difficult it is to read his handwriting, not to mention those entire pages written in pencil which time has half erased and can only be read, line by line, either slanted a certain way towards a lamp, or with a magnifying glass. Those problems can be solved, however; the worst are certain letters that could have been written the same way: for example, *p* and *q* or *p* and *f,* or *n, u,* and a double *s,* or even *a* and *o*. Since he did not regularly dot his *i*s or use accents, *n* and *si,* or *m* and *rri* are easily confused. I could go on forever, listing the snags I keep coming across. Another example is the articles *le* and *la* which are impossible to differentiate. This is not important if the substantive noun that follows seems certain, but it leads to confusion if one is not sure. Peter Handke has written a novel which I haven't read, but whose title I remember: *The Goalie's Anxiety at the Penalty Kick*. I assure you his anxiety can't be any worse than mine when I must decide between *queue* and *guerre,* for example. This is perhaps an extreme case and, fortunately for me, an exception, but if I am sometimes unsure, even slightly, I know that I will have to begin the procedure all over again. I will have to go back to the scribbler and make another draft in a few months. Little by little the text becomes alive, the meaning appears as if from within, something is triggered and not only am I no longer desperate, but I have the impression that I have finally succeeded in both reading and understanding the text. Generally, a step-by-step reading is the one that makes the most sense. It's as if, from layer to layer, from the accumulation of work, I earn the right to understand. If, in addition to the numerous drafts, one adds the several readings required in preparing the text for the editor, as well as the corrections made on the first and second proofs one would have to say that each scribbler is totally revised at least six or seven times. I live amidst pages covered with signs; either manuscript pages, typed and corrected pages, or printed pages. I sometimes have nightmares where different letters jostle one another just to torment me. A particularly difficult reading or part of a resistant sentence will follow me in my sleep. My anxiety is so great at times that Antonin Artaud appears in my dreams, reproaching me for not having understood him.

What kind of life have I had from being in contact almost every moment with the texts of Antonin Artaud, the written substance of his life? Inasmuch as I tried to keep a certain distance and tried to detach myself in order to preserve the accuracy that his work demanded, my life has been haunted by him. Nothing is stranger to me than imitation, which seems contrary to loyalty, a loyalty which was asked of me in 1947. In spite of my attempts at distance and detachment, it was, however, necessary to retrace his footsteps more than once; for example, I had to find out for myself how the tarot worked, or read what he had once read in order to know to what he was alluding.

All of my intellectual faculty, should I have any, was used so Antonin Artaud's work would be known. That lone preoccupation earned me a rather ascetic solitary existence. I didn't really live in the world. It's as if my life had stopped at one particular moment in time, as if I had stopped time. Was my getting old only a feeling? Part of me still responds as if I were the young woman Antonin Artaud welcomed in his room at Ivry. Enlivened by the same passion, that young woman did not see time go by, but the other one knows that the years have accumulated, and that her body is not without organs and, unfortunately, breaks down a little more each day.

Has the time of reckoning come? With volume XXI which has just appeared I have succeeded in publishing the whole of the scribblers from Rodez. I feel irritated when I hear myself say that the reading of this enormous body of work is discouraging. I don't overlook that it is difficult, but I compare it to the determination that allowed them to see the light of day. I also know that the challenge presented by these thousands of pages is necessary in order to understand the extraordinary process of a man wrenching himself from his own alienation.

My fear is that I no longer have enough time. Will I fail so close to my goal? Will senility, death, intervene before I've published the last scribbler? All distractions, all activities that veer me away from my main project feel like violations. I even feel guilty taking these few hours to write this letter in order to accede to the request of Frans De Haes. Was I successful? Did I truly accomplish what he expected of me?

I could have condensed the whole undertaking in a few lines: I knew a man named Antonin Artaud who was approximately fifty years old. I then lived with his work and learned to know another Antonin Artaud. I knew him, yet I also knew someone else. He was, at times, twenty years old, and at other times he was a mature man. I met him in Ireland, in Mexico, at Ville-Évrard, and at Rodez. I was hoping to be able to say one day that my work was finished, and that at last I could, like anyone else, read Antonin

Artaud and get to know yet another Antonin Artaud. I have only been able to do this very rarely when, taking a break from deciphering, restructuring, preparing, correcting proofs, I pick up one of the volumes from *Oeuvres complètes* of Antonin Artaud and begin to read, forgetting the small role I played in its publication. A marvelous discovery which is renewed each time.

One more word, dear Bernard. One day, many years ago, when I was speaking to Jean Genêt about this wonderful gift that had been given me, he replied that it was a poisoned gift. By this I understand he meant that my life has been weighed down by its solitude. But I am almost certain that he was wrong. Not even death would know how to quench the ardour Antonin Artaud left me.

With much affection.
Paris, January 29, 1986

Florence de Mèredieu:
A Review of *L'Affaire Artaud*

If someone were to ask me which writers have most influenced my writing the name of Antonin Artaud would never occur to me yet I have at least a dozen books of his sitting on my shelves between Hubert Aquin and Margaret Avison. I have, over the years, given away dozens of boxes of books to university libraries, second-hand bookstores, Value Village—books I know I will never read or consult again—but never Antonin Artaud's. Or Paule Thévenin's. She sits on my shelves between Sharon Thesen and Tzvetan Todorov.

In reading Benoît Peeters's biography, *Derrida*, published by Flammarion in 2010, I came across Paule Thévenin's name several times. Derrida admired and wrote extensively on Artaud's work and solicited Thévenin's opinion on many issues relating to Artaud. This led to friendship and collaborations involving Artaud's work, including his drawings and sketches. Peeters reports a few incidents suggesting that Thévenin was not always the easiest person with whom to get along. In fact, I'd read that following her death, several friends reported in newspapers such as *Libération* and *Le Monde* that she was "terribly different" and had an "extraordinary talent of an '*emmerdeuse*,'" a shit-disturber. It did not surprise me. Anyone with the tenacity and devotion she exhibited over the course of forty-seven years working on Artaud's manuscripts has to have unshakable convictions on many fronts and in many situations. In any event, anyone aware of Artaud's antisocial mindset would understand the necessity of having one "shit-disturber" work on another "shit-disturber's" opus.

I found it strange that in his biography, Peeters did not mention Florence de Mèredieu, a writer who has written at least six books and several articles on Artaud and is also a vociferous critic of both Thévenin and Derrida. I assumed that, like so many literary and journalistic venues in France, Peeters preferred to ignore Florence de Mèredieu, at least in his *Derrida* biography. He does, however, mention her briefly in a diary he kept while writing the biography, *Trois ans avec Derrida Les carnets d'un biographe*, published by Flammarion in 2010. As brief and cryptic as those references were, they nevertheless roused my curiosity. Who exactly was this woman, Florence de Mèredieu? I decided to look into rumours I'd heard or read about her obsession with Paule Thévenin and ordered a few of her books. The following is a review of Mèredieu's *L'Affaire Artaud: Journal ethnographique*, published by Fayard in 2009, sixteen years after Paule Thévenin's death in 1993, and five years after Jacques Derrida's in 2004. The English translations of the quotes are mine.

Because the book stands at six-hundred-and-eighty pages, one would assume that Mèredieu's ethnographic journal, as the title claims it to be, would offer an extensive cultural examination of what has become known as the "Artaud affair," a long and controversial history around the publication of Artaud's work. It does not. One would also assume that a book of such length and of such potentially cultural significance would have been edited for repetition. It couldn't have been. I stopped counting early on how many times Mèredieu calls Thévenin malicious names. The following are but a few examples repeated throughout the book: "Great Guru," a name she also assigns to Derrida; "Great Goddess;" "Sentinel." Artaud, in fact, dedicated a drawing he made of Thévenin with the following: "I place my daughter as sentinel."

While this may be viewed as a generous and grateful gesture on Artaud's part, Mèredieu uses the dedication as another opportunity for derision. She also refers to Thévenin as a "vestal." I presume this means she sees Thévenin as a virginal Vesta, keeper of Artaud's flame. The list goes on: "Great Priestess; "Grand Pythoness," a term normally used to brand women as being possessed and speaking through another's spirit. Does "*Mater Dolorosa*" imply that Thévenin saw herself as the sorrowful mother of Christ/Artaud? Or is it simply another example of Mèredieu's unremitting imagination? She also refers to Thévenin as "shaman," "Great Medium," "protective tigress," "virtuous one," ad nauseum. At one point, Mèredieu wonders what kind of life "this novice" Thévenin could possibly have had without the Artaud project, insinuating that she had no other talent or interest. Strange insinuation given that Thévenin had, by the time she met Artaud in her early twenties completed her course work in medicine plus two years of internship in psychiatry. She must have had something to offer the long list of renowned friends who congregated at her house on a regular basis: Arthur Adamov, Jean Genêt, Pierre Boulez, Francis Ponge, Roger Blin, Pierre Klossowski, Michel Leiris, Marguerite and Jacques Derrida, Julia Kristeva, Philippe Sollers. Mèredieu facetiously refers to Sollers as "Comrade" several times because of his Marxist leanings, another opportunity she simply couldn't resist. It was at Paule and Yves Thévenin's apartment that Jean Genêt and Jacques Derrida became good friends. It was on the basis of this friendship that Derrida wrote *Glas*, a complex text that plays on variations between literary texts such as Genêt's and philosophical ones as Hegel's. According to Mèredieu, all these highly creative people who also happened to be friends of Thévenin had simply fallen under the spell of the Great Guru. It would appear that the so-called "guru novice" might have been more remarkable than Mèredieu could fathom or even understand.

Florence de Mèredieu loves to postulate and never misses an opportunity to do so. At the point when Thévenin had been working on Artaud's manuscripts for thirty-three-years, Mèredieu wonders if perhaps Thévenin's followers might have perceived her as a "Christ-like" figure given the thirty-three years that she had, thus far, worked on Artaud's scribblers. It doesn't seem to matter to Mèredieu that Thévenin deciphered, transcribed and edited Artaud's work for forty-seven years, from 1946 until her death in 1993. Mèredieu chooses to focus on the thirty-third year. Needless to say this doesn't make sense, yet her book is full of these exaggerated extrapolations. She even proposes that Thévenin may have seen herself as the heroine of a legendary couple, Paule as Juliet to Artaud's Romeo... Paule's Isolde to Artaud's Tristan... She then decides that these references may be too flattering or high-minded and compares their relationship to a story reminiscent of a cheap Harlequin novelette... Not facts, but suppositions.

One fact that Mèredieu doesn't fail to remind us of over and over again—sometimes two or three times per page—is that she is an intellectual academic and as such she holds a privileged position from which she can better read and understand the work of Antonin Artaud. She makes clear and unflattering distinctions between people who are intellectual academics like herself, and people who are not and accuses Thévenin of not fully understanding Artaud because of her lack of academic and intellectual background. She neglects to point out that many, if not most, of those who gathered at Paule and Yves Thévenin's apartment were not academics, and those who were happened to be highly creative.

Why does Mèredieu constantly refer to Thévenin's transcription and editing of four-hundred-and-six scribblers as a hoax, a fraud? Mainly because Thévenin dared change the *position* of certain lines from the scribblers to the published books. As Thévenin explained in her letter above, there were also circumstances when she had to make editorial decisions based on Artaud's penmanship and the first-draft quality of the scribblers. It might be true, as Mèredieu believes, that Artaud was a genius whose first drafts should have been published "to the letter, to the comma, to the line," but it is also true that he was often under great mental and physical stress and as such his work was deserving of close editorial attention. One of Mèredieu's main complaints is that in Volume XXVI, Thévenin assembled notes that Artaud had made for a particular conference which was to take place in January 1947 at the Théâtre du Vieux-Colombier. These particular notes were dispersed amongst different scribblers, presumably written down as ideas occurred to him. As Thévenin explains in her notes in the back of this particular volume, the different projects he was working on over the course of several scribblers differed greatly in tone and subject and it was decided to assemble the notes for this conference as a complete volume instead of having them scattered in different volumes as they appeared in the scribblers. This would seem to be a completely valid substantive editing decision, but not to Mèredieu. According to her, the scribblers edited by Thévenin were transcribed by "a possessed woman" mainly for the "pseudo-theoretical and pseudo-intellectual." In other words, for people who are not academics. I fail to understand her reasoning since all published books go through a substantive editorial process involving content, organization, design and style in order to make a document more functional. The process is mostly analysis-based and requires editorial judgement which, unlike copyediting, does not rely on application of rules. A process which, I may add, would have greatly benefitted Mèredieu's own book.

"Les gens ont peur..." People are afraid, Mèredieu insists in an effort to make Thévenin and her supporters powerful enough to destroy careers, including hers. She constantly refers to open letters she wrote to newspapers that were never published. She complains about the lack of reviews for her published books due, supposedly, to Thévenin's power, even twenty years after her death. In fact, there is so much paranoia running throughout this book it leaves the impression that the writer suffers from a severe imbalance of judgement. There were many negative reviews of *L'Affaire Artaud* following its publication in 2009, one whose caption reads: "Pour en finir avec le jugement de Mèredieu." To have done with the judgement of Mèredieu, a take on Artaud's famous recording *Pour en finir avec le jugement de Dieu*: To have done with the judgement of God. Mèredieu has posted frenzied responses to these reviews on her blog and claims to have simply told the truth. Considering that her ethnographic journal repeatedly asks if she is the only one "to have seen the truth, to have seen that the empress [Thévenin] has no clothes," one wonders if, in fact, she is capable of objective analysis.

No one escapes Mèredieu's disparagement: the publisher, Gallimard, is mocked mainly for allowing Thévenin to edit Artaud's work; Serge Mallauséna, Artaud's nephew, with whom Mèredieu initially shared "secrets" and "an antipathy for Thévenin." She forgives him his lack of intellect because of his great "instinct" as he solicits her opinion on several issues which Mèredieu gives with great enthusiasm. Eventually, however, she notices that he distances himself, does not share his contacts or open his own archives to her and she wonders if she hasn't helped him too much. When he receives accolades from the press and aligns himself with Gallimard for a new edition of his uncle's work, Mèredieu accuses him of falling under the spell of the powerful establishment and sees him merely as a Thévenin replacement.

Another source for Mèredieu's disparagement is Évelyne Grossman. Again, Mèredieu is initially enthusiastic about Grossman's plans to publish a second edition of Artaud's scribblers, but her enthusiasm is somewhat tempered when she reads the new edition and Grossman's acknowledgement and admiration of Thévenin's work. Her keenness is mitigated even more when she learns that Grossman's version has also been "edited" and is not rendered exactly as the scribblers, "to the letter, to the comma, to the line." This new edition, she asserts, is a perfect example of "Jesuitism," a distortion and misrepresentation. Accordingly, only a specialist and informed intellectual as herself can fully appreciate what is amiss in Grossman's edition. As such, this edition, titled *Quatro*, can only be viewed as an "intermediary" version until such time as someone publishes all four-hundred-and-six scribblers as they were written, along with the integrated, sketches, drawings, doodles, etc... Her resentment becomes more palpable as Grossman is viewed as the new Artaud specialist.

Mèredieu seems to run into problems with just about anyone with whom she has contact. She describes her relationship with the Georges Pompidou Centre as "thorny." Or when she proposes a project to the Louvre but never receives a response. When she researches the Artaud archives at the National Library she complains that a member of the staff is assigned to keep watch over her. The list goes on.

I was never so glad to come to the end of a book. I wanted to put it down well before its last pages, but because I had decided to write a review I was required to read all of it. The last fifty pages consist mostly of more name-calling, especially when it comes to Jacques Derrida. I am not an unreserved Derrida admirer, but another litany of names—"Great Initiate, Ventriloquist, Great Manitou, God Himself, Pope," does wear on one's patience. In labelling him "*sacripant*" does Mèredieu mean that Derrida is a scoundrel, a bully, a braggart? Even if he were all of these things, what does this have to do with his work? She faults him for not being analytical enough in an academic sense, but academic analysis was precisely what Derrida did not want to do. It was the main reason he could not obtain a higher position on the French academic ladder. It is ironic that his work reminds Mèredieu of "the compulsive and repetitive rituals of neurosis," considering her own compulsion to repeat. She favours work, including hers, which deals with research, archives, historical traces, what she designates as "the real." It is, once again, a curious statement considering Mèredieu is also a visual art critic. Yet, she seems to draw an unbreachable line between creativity in language and creativity in the visual arts.

There are many "ifs" that went into the making of Mèredieu's "ethnographic journal" that could have resulted in a better book: if she had addressed some of the questions she brings up in a professional manner without endless accusations of "hoax and fraud;" if she had given specific examples and references to her claims instead of three or four examples of supposed irregularities from volume XXVI—irregularities explained by Thévenin in forty-fives pages of "Notes" at the end of this volume, as she did with all the volumes she edited; if Mèredieu had held back the numerous accusations flung at just about everyone she meets, etc., her book might have had some credibility. It does not. She claims not to understand the inflated rumours swirling around her, or where all the "caricatural, carnivalesque and neurotic portrayals" come from. For answers I would suggest she read her own *L'Affaire Artaud*.

I would like to end with a quote—my translation—from Antonin Artaud, in *Oeuvres complètes XXVI*:

> ...
> and I thought that this lengthy pursuit of a man by
> some kind of bad destiny was not the pursuit of a man
> by destiny
> but of a man by men, by a group of determined men,
> and it looked terribly like a story by the initiates.
> Only the hatred of initiates can go on for so long and is so desperate,
> but what in hell do I have to do with initiates? me,
> A.

Mistaken Identity:
Plenary Speaking

Although many years have gone by since I delivered an early draft of the following essay as a talk at a conference, I think the subject of identity is still as relevant now as it was then, perhaps even more so. My first impulse when I was invited to give a plenary talk at the annual meeting of the Association of Canadian and Québec Literatures was to turn it down. I was busy with overdue projects and planning trips but mainly I questioned why a writer of non-academic texts, a sometimes poet, sometimes-novelist, sometimes-translator, would be speaking to an audience made up mostly of academics. Could someone have made a mistake? *Quelqu'un aurait peut-être commis une erreur sur ma personne?* There have been many situations when I have asked myself the question: what am I doing here? It is less an ontological or philosophical question than a feeling of dislocation.

Before declining the invitation from the ACQL, however, I looked up its website and the focus of the conference: Paradoxes of Citizenship: Environments, Exclusions, Equity. The call for papers suggested possible topics:

> Identity, vulnerability, and exclusion
> Fragmented identities and fragmented textualities
> Cultural identities, cultural canons and literary forms
> Reconsidering borders: territories, cultures, canons and identities
> Masculine identities and textualities.

The long list of possible identities did little to convince me until I conveyed my reservations to an academic friend who remarked in a dismissive manner that the topic of identity had been addressed extensively in academic circles over the last few years and it was now outdated. It struck me how easily concepts, constructs and theories come into vogue only to be discarded as yesterday's topics. Concepts, constructs and theories should be agents of change, yet they are so easily disposed of without having exercised much influence other than serving as trendy subjects for papers at conferences. This probably explains why the suggested topics listed above did not include feminine or feminist identities. While the topic has hardly been exhausted, it is tired—tired perhaps from having spoken so forcefully within certain circles without the achievement of everything to which its speakers aspired. It is a fate that the topic of masculine identities will soon meet if it hasn't already. It was already tired in the '90s when Elizabeth Badinter, French feminist philosopher, published *XY: On Masculine Identity*. It examines the changing masculine role models from flesh and blood cowboy of the 1950s to the machine-like Terminator of the '90s, and she suggests that it is now time for new constructs and new models with which men can identify.

I, personally, have never known blood and flesh cowboys or, for that matter, men who model themselves after them. True, I went to Saturday afternoon matinees as a child and did see cowboys on screen, but even then I perceived them—at the level of a child's subconscious perhaps—as mythical characters and not, as Badinter suggests, as flesh and blood men. As for the machine-like model of the Terminator, again I personally don't know any, although there is ample evidence that there are men who would like to model themselves after such a figure.

If, as Elizabeth Badinter suggests, new masculine models have to be constructed with which men can identify, my first question would be: will they, like the cowboy and the Terminator, be based on fantasies grounded in forms of external reality with little grounding in historical events or interpretations of memory? If the myths of the past failed us to such an extent that we have to keep inventing new ones, who is going to spawn them and according to what guidelines? Who is going to impose those guidelines? Do social philosophers such as Badinter believe that this kind of instrumental thinking—based on the untenable hypothesis of agent-means-ends—accounts for most human practices? Badinter's hypothesis may mean well but it seems to leave out a major part of human experience, namely inter-subjective relations between *real* people, unlike her proposition, which seems to involve mainly stereotypes. It sounds like yet another philosopher taking on an entire segment of the population because she deems it in dire need of remodeling.

I understand the need for social groups to engage in struggles for the recognition of their particular interests. The historical development of identity politics arose out of and as a negation of mass social movements. The National Liberation Movement and Civil Rights Movement in the United States emphasized common interests and alliances in opposition to external powers. Movements such as the Women's Liberation Movement were largely responsible for introducing elements of personal politics and interpersonal relations to identity politics.

As important as these movements were, the focus on and the compounding of perceived differences within and outside various groups often yielded strange results. As more people began to think of themselves as oppressed minorities, the lines between the oppressed and the oppressors were often blurred. Some groups, in an attempt to preserve their boundaries, isolated themselves while others polarized themselves in the privileging of one group over another. Isolation and polarization offered limited and provisional solutions depending on who was dominating the stage at any one time, each trend an attempt to dominate for a few seasons. I have been reminded of this many times when reading daily newspapers on the growing number of fundamentalist developments. Why do Canadians so easily accept anti-female religious and cultural attitudes imported into Canada? Are they doing so in order to protect the rights of other identity-based cultures and religions regardless of their attitudes towards women? Are equal rights mainly for Western, mostly white, mostly upper- and middle-class educated women? Has the academic left, via Michel Foucault, the principal philosophical spokesperson for Identity Politics, been stressing the socially constructed identity of cultural groups while obliviously feeding right-wing nationalist, fundamentalist and racist ideologies? Why are there still so many reports of abuse, violence and demeaning behaviour against women? While Canadian women have made some inroads over the last fifty years, why is there still so much sexist advertising in the glossy magazines that come with the *Globe and Mail* or *Toronto Life* or other magazines and newspapers? Did the value of "femininity" change significantly as a result of the various feminist narratives of the last century?

In her now outdated book, *The New Feminism,* the British writer Natasha Walter points out that the reason old-style feminism failed is that it may have concentrated too much on personal and psychological issues at the expense of larger, more unyielding political and economic problems. Old-style feminism, according to Walter, may have paid too much attention to how women dress and talk at the expense of confronting the real challenges of inequality and equality. She is confident that a new feminism will replace the politically correct idealism of the old with the political and economic power of a new feminism in order to better address inequality between the sexes. What Natasha Walter doesn't tell us, however, is how she defines equality and inequality. It has been my observation in the last few decades that the over-determined values of what is equal and powerful in our culture are not always sought out by women. What role does this play in the definition of equality?

In spite of what Natasha Walter has written about old-style feminists having concentrated too much on the personal , I will, to a certain extent, make myself the subject of this talk according to one of the many definitions of *identity* in the OED: "The condition or fact of a person or thing being that specified unique person or thing"—a definition I prefer to: "the quality or condition of being identical to another." According to this latter definition, in order to belong to a group that is identity-based, one has to be identically exemplary.

So why, I ask once again, was a non-academic invited to speak on a supposedly outdated subject as "identity?" Could it have to do with my own assumed identity crisis because I write in a language that is not my mother tongue? I speak French and English but I write mostly in English which is not my mother tongue. When I first began to write I assumed I would be writing in French but every time I tried I became literally aphasic.

A few years back I was invited to present a paper in French at a conference on the subject of *De l'art à la culture... l'intimité dans la diversité*. I accepted mainly because of the word *diversité*. As I began to write I soon realized that I would have to write the paper in English first, then, with the help of a translator, compile a French version. The paper took at least three times longer to write than if I had written and delivered it in English, but I felt that the last stage, my own French translation of a translation, played with its own non-identity which appealed to me. Until its actual presentation. As good as my spoken French is I felt I did not belong on this panel. It was yet another occasion when I found myself wondering what I was doing on a panel made up of two well-known French-speaking actors from Québec, a French-speaking poet from Acadia, and a Native playwright from Ontario who wrote mainly in English. Except for the Native playwright whose identity could not—would not—be questioned no matter what language he spoke or wrote in, I was the least *Francophone* there. This panel was not, as I had expected, as diversified as the name of the conference suggested. As I listened to claims of assured identity, the need to belong to a tribe with strong cultural roots, roots which to me have always seemed as mythological as the cowboy and the Terminator figures who were more folkloric than real, it occurred to me that not only did I not belong to a tribe or to this panel, I did not, in fact, belong to any specific group. I no longer belonged to a time when I could identify myself strictly as a Francophone, if ever there was such a time. My mother tongue, transplanted or lost, was not now, nor had it ever been exemplary. *Je n'écris pas un Français exemplaire. Je ne suis pas Française ou Québécoise, je suis une Franco-Ontarienne qui écrit dans une langue qui n'est pas la sienne.* I am what one person on the panel called me, *une assimilée.* He also accused me of being *une traître*, a traitor, but I'm not going to bother addressing this. Suffice it to say that I have indeed been partially assimilated into another culture, another language.

 I write mainly in English, but the language in which I write is never at one with itself. Because of my background, whenever I speak either French or English I am always an *other*, each language a stranger to the other, each language a stranger to itself.

 My first novel, *Frog Moon*, treats the dilemma of a character faced with writing in a language that is not her mother tongue. Although it generally received good reviews—one critic described it as a Franco-Ontarian novel written in English—another critic reviewing the French translation referred to it as *un roman d'accommodement*, a novel of compromise. He also lifted, out of context, a quote from an interview where I supposedly said that I had chosen to write in English over French when, in fact, I had said that the choice was between writing in English or not writing at all. There is a difference. Not writing at all would have been the compromise. Writing in the language in which I was most comfortable was not. The affirmation of an otherness, of not belonging, of feeling dislocated, I gladly assume through writing. Kafka once declared that it was impossible for him to write in Czech, in Yiddish or in German, yet it was impossible for him *not* to write. In fact, mastering a language other than one's mother tongue is an assertive gesture especially vis-à-vis those who too readily accommodate themselves to the easy logic of categories such as assimilation, treachery, identities and compromise.

I like to tell the story of George Steiner who was brought up speaking four languages—German, Yiddish, French and English. He spoke all four fluently and when he began to write he yearned to know what his true mother tongue was so he went to a German analyst who put him under hypnosis. The analyst spoke to Steiner in German and, under hypnosis, Steiner answered in German. He then went to a second hypnotist who spoke French and Steiner, under hypnosis, answered in French. The same thing happened when he went to English and Jewish hypnotists, Steiner answered in English and Yiddish. All this is to say that perhaps we speak, at any given time, the language that listens to us. *Peut-être parlons-nous la langue qui nous écoute.* The two times I submitted French manuscripts to French publishers in Canada they have been returned with encouraging remarks, but no offer of publication yet I have always found publishers for manuscripts written primarily in English. *Peut-être écrivons nous dans la langue qui nous lit?*

What may be perceived in my case as an identity crisis is, in fact, not a crisis at all. After having answered for the hundredth time: "Why did you abandon your mother tongue," it occurred to me that in cases of abandonment it isn't the child who abandons the mother, it is the mother who abandons the child. I didn't abandon my mother tongue; it abandoned me. Language is inherited and my inheritance never came through. I would go as far as to say that it didn't come through because it was, literally, illiterate. Illiterate because it was the language of a childhood spent partly in an English neighbourhood in Northern Ontario and partly in a convent where students were confined to silence or prayers for the greater part of the day. Illiterate because the teachers were nuns who had joined their religious order when they were barely sixteen and, for the most part, were poorly educated themselves; illiterate because the books that could have been the most beneficial to the students were censored. The main function of being raised a Catholic when I was growing up was not to educate liberally but to mold children to Catholic thinking. Perhaps Catholic education has changed since then—I don't keep track—but this is how it was then; this was my inheritance.

I was stupefied to discover while living in France in the seventies, a period of great political and intellectual ferment, that I could barely understand the French books I was buying and reading. Yet, it would have been politically incorrect in French Canada to have said so. It probably still is. I now have rows of books written in French with their English translations by their side. My own early books of poetry were interpreted as having been written in English because my French had been oppressed by an external power, namely the English language. It was the popular victim-oriented accusation at the time and, again, it would have been politically incorrect to point out that perhaps the oppressing power was not entirely external. I believe it was Gilles Deleuze who pointed out that speaking a language that is not one's own is rooted within the memory of an unchosen identity and cannot be reduced to the decisional act of an abstract will. I did not decide or choose to write mostly in English. It chose me.

For the first part of my life in Northern Ontario I spoke, to paraphrase Gilles Deleuze, a "minor language," a French idiom that did not exist in writing. What Deleuze defines as the speakers of a minor language supposes a people born of a deterritorialization which, far from rooting them in one place, one identity, one memory, releases them from borders. Deleuze, in fact, in departing from the assumptions of the classical contract theory of societies, pointed to the violence inherent in identity and the partialities to clan or nation.

From an early age, while speaking a "minor language" as defined by Deleuze, I moved into a language that was not my own and explored it, until I realized that my self-identities, the concepts of my identities, had broken down. While many people around me strove to be the best examples of Franco-Ontarians, the best feminists, the best poets, novelists and academics, I was not an exemplary model for any of these. The prototypical movements that bring together like-minded artists, like-minded thinkers, like-minded feminists or religious believers, were, as far as I was concerned, falling apart. I wrote mainly in English but I wasn't a true Anglophone. I wasn't less than an Anglophone; in fact, because I also spoke French, I may have been a little more. I was a Franco-Ontarian whose main body of work was not in French, but I didn't feel less of a Franco-Ontarian, I felt a little more. I was a mother but because I was also a writer, I wasn't less of a mother, I was a little more. As poet, novelist, translator, essayist, I was always a little less and a little more. What each identity had in common with the other was also what distinguished and differentiated it from the other. What I have in common with another Franco-Ontarian is the fact that we are not the same. Being Franco-Ontarian is never brought to an exemplary completion; nor is writing as an Anglo-Ontarian. And, might I add, one of the advantages of getting on in years is the discovery that identity is no longer contingent on one organizing principle over the course of a lifetime. Growth is not linear, nor does it necessarily proceed in successive stages. How one approaches the world as one ages becomes both simpler and more complex. With each passing year I find myself adopting and discarding identities, not necessarily as a consequence of any sense of progression or development, but according to my own whims and changing interests. As youth abandons me, I move forward and backward as I collect a life's symbols and meanings from which to create—and discard—roles that never quite defined who I was or who I am. The more identity breaks down, the more it consists of not being identical to anyone, not even to one's self.

When people still find it necessary to ask why I abandoned my mother tongue, I am reminded of the French philosopher, Jean-Luc Nancy, who points out in *The Birth to Presence* that the word "abandon" evokes "abundance." There is always abundance in abandonment as it opens onto a profusion of possibilities, just as one abandons oneself to excess, for there is no other modality of abandon. The abandoned being finds itself returned to the abundance that it was for it has no other identity than its default of identity.

Nancy's take on abandonment and abundance reminds me of Derrida's concept of the supplement. The term "mother tongue" was originally associated with the fixed cultural model of an originary mother. But it isn't unusual for children nowadays to have what Derrida refers to as "supplements" of mothers. Marriages and relationships collapse and children inherit stepmothers and stepfathers; gay couples adopt or find surrogate mothers for egg donors. Donor eggs can be fertilized in tubes, transplanted into surrogate wombs and delivered to a third mother. The configurations seem endless depending on whether the couple is gay or lesbian. There are families where the father is more mothering than the mother. It wasn't long ago, within certain social circles, when servants, wet nurses, nannies raised the children instead of the birth mother. Cloning may soon become part of the picture. The point I am belabouring is that the role of the mother can no longer be reduced to that of one genetrix. Considering mothers can have adjuncts, why can't mother tongues?

Over the years, my writing has been criticized as being either "essentialist feminist writing" or "language-focused writing reminiscent of a white male elite." My point is not to pinpoint contradictory claims of criticism, but to emphasize that writers should not be expected to contract forms of social insurance or, what I call co-operative writing, that which co-operates with what is expected of it. I used to think of co-operative writing as literature that catered mainly to popular taste until I noticed its prescriptive head rearing at the other end of the writing spectrum: small groups of so-called avant-garde or non-representational or experimental writers who look down on writing that does not follow their guidelines, while their own writing evolves into theatres of stereotype by consciously or unconsciously taking on the scripted model of the group. As in so many other fields, over-determined values play an important role in how we identify and separate ourselves from others. It always reminds me of some expedient distilling process by which writers are extracted, plucked, remodeled, distilled in order to make them fit into tight, claustrophobic categories until they become reduced versions of who they are or could be.

We interpret identity to mean a belonging together. If we think of belonging together in the customary way, it is determined by the word "together" that is, by its unity. To belong means to be assigned and placed into an order of "togetherness," combined into the unity of a system mediated by the unifying centre of some authoritative synthesis. Philosophy, namely via Heidegger, represents this belonging as *nexus* and *connexion,* the necessary connection of the one with the other. It is a necessary connection as long as it does not impose itself and dictate how each individual should think, write, or be. Unfortunately, this prevailing belonging is often misunderstood as a connection that must be established for the good of the community. What is a community Jean-Luc

Nancy asks in *Being Singular Plural*? His answer is grim. Community does not necessarily mean one big happy family:

> Being with, being together, being "united" are precisely not a matter of being "one." Within the unitary community there is nothing but death, death found in the ashes of crematorium ovens... To put it in another way: in a paradigmatic manner, the systematic rape of Bosnian women deployed all the various figures of this delirious affirmation of a "unitary" community: rape in order to beget bastards... (not children but bastards) who are excluded a priori from the assumed unity: rape so that this repeated act assigns its victims to the fantasy unity of a community. Rape in order to show in every possible way that there does not have to be relations between communities. Rape is the zero act. It is the negation of all relation, the negation of the child, the negation of woman. It is pure affirmation of the rapist in whom a pure identity finds nothing better than submission to what it denies: relation and being-together.

What a different picture this paints from an abundance or a *supplement* of mothers! As Nancy also points out a pure identity always cancels itself out because it can no longer identify itself. No one was ever pure enough to be an Aryan worthy of the name. We know that this question could drive a true Nazi...to suicide. Why am I bringing up these old claims of Aryan purity? Because, in one form or another, they simply never went away. The concept of racial purity is, of course, nothing more than an *idea*, an abstraction. I've never known anyone with a "pure" pedigree, nor have I ever known anyone who can agree on what that *idea* is. Maybe it has to do with stereotypes. I'm often surprised that English translations of Michel Tremblay's plays are so popular in Anglophone Toronto. When I have asked English-speaking Torontonians why this is, I realize that many of Tremblay's characters reinforce stereotypes that Anglo Torontonians hold to this day. They are fascinated by the *idea* of a *Québécois* in much the same way many are fascinated by the *idea* of Native people without personally knowing any.

One of the poets I most admire is Paul Celan. His is a poetry of witnessing—witnessing the universal as an absolute singularity, as the other and in the name of the other as stranger. George Steiner once wrote that the enigma of Auschwitz could only be penetrated in German, the language of death itself. Celan wrote primarily in German, the language of those who murdered his parents. In appropriating the murderers' language, he widened the narrow space of easy categories. He opened up the fertile ground of complex relationships that develop when issues are not reduced to simple polarities and antitheses. In exceeding the simple opposition between aggressor and victim, in moving with the German language in order to create exceptionally fine poetry, Celan created an event beyond simple identities, a multiplicity and a migration of language and country beyond borders. As Derrida points out in *Sovereignties in Question: The Poetics of Paul Celan*, because of his poetics Celan left a mark that counters the German language, approaches it, reaches it, but never surrenders to it.

To move within another's language is a mark of *universal* exemplarity, even for those who have not experienced circumstances as tragic as Celan's. This is not to say that we should all speak one universal language or that we should erase all differences, but rather that we should disassociate languages, idioms, and differences from extreme nationalism and other isms. Celan inherited and mastered the German language and left his personal mark on it so his art could live on.

While fascism unleashed its hatred and wreaked havoc on the world, Heidegger worked on formulations of the principle of identity and differences, one of the highest principles of Western thought. Heard in its fundamental key, Heidegger's equation states that the unity of identity forms a basic characteristic in the Being of beings. Everywhere, wherever and however we are related to beings of every kind, identity makes its claim on us. If these claims were not made, Heidegger asserts, human beings would never appear fully in their Being. It is, indeed, a noble *idea*. Unfortunately it was being formulated around the time Heidegger was turning over his Jewish colleagues—flesh and blood colleagues—to the Nazi machine, the perfect model of the Terminator. Knowledge, it would seem, is not always of great service to men and women of knowledge.

I am not suggesting that we do away with identity altogether; it would be impossible. Individual and collective identities are essential to social existence. There is comfort to be found in history, memory, tradition, all of which serve to consolidate who we are if consolidation is what we aspire to. Undoubtedly, this is why collective self-seeking is so popular. In spite of growing tolerance for diversity, there still exists a basic need to know where each individual belongs. Guidelines for being are more comforting than looking to uncertainty. However, when collective identity overrides the essential democratic values of the individual, it has exceeded its bounds. It is true that a society which is not defined by a clear or a traditional identity will lose a certain amount of social cohesion. In a democracy which guarantees the autonomy of the individual, social interaction will sometimes have to be sacrificed.

Perhaps the best way to be faithful to a heritage is to be unfaithful to it, not to accept it literally as a totality, but rather to grasp its dogmatic moments, its prohibitions, its laws and limits. Too often, in our desperate need to validate who we are, we anchor thought, we secure symbolic functions instead of questioning and decentring them as many artists and writers do in their work.

One of the reasons I was attracted to Derrida's concept of *différance*—I'm aware that he didn't call it a concept nor do I fully understand it—was because he interrupted and delimited laws and called into question any identity that found shelter in them. It was undoubtedly one of the main reasons he met with much resistance within the conservative and traditional French academic world, especially within philosophy departments. Questioning and uncertainty are not features of the masterful. And yes, I'm aware of the irony since Derrida himself conducted himself as a master, as I witnessed in two of his seminars. But while some may feel safer within the havens of fewer choices, they reduce ways of seeing and thinking. When cultural, philosophical, sexual, and racial complexities are reduced to a binary ledger of "I am this which is superior to what I am not," life may seem more certain and simple. Unfortunately, the more interesting story may well be happening in a more diverse space of uncertainty.

We have seen, in the last few decades, how the *parti Québécois* and various offshoots, in their ceaseless searches for self-definition, as witnessed in a recent proposed charter of values, exemplify how politics can be reduced to narrowly defined identities in order to manipulate and strengthen opinions within identity groups. Politics that misunderstand the sublimation of conflicts, whether they are based on language, ethnicity, religion or sexual orientation, always run the risk of being overturned by clashes representing the other language, the other ethnicity, the other religion, the other sexuality, etc... It leaves little opportunity for arbitration, compromise or plurality. Plurality, which insures the autonomy of the individual, has its foundation in the separation of church and state as launched by William of Ockham, but it can be applied to other domains as well. Politicians should be reminded of what Ockham had in mind—the separation of domains, not the triumph or privileging of one over the other. The basic principle of the separation of various domains such as politics and church, or between public and private life, should mirror the distinction between collective and individual identity. Yet, in the name of patriotism, we are expected to agree on issues such as war and religion. We are expected to adhere to party lines. Women are expected to agree with one another simply because we are women. Just as personal autonomy does not derive from the autonomy of the collective, so the world of personal relations should remain distinct from the relations that exist between people by virtue of living together in one society.

It isn't easy; it is likely quite messy. The personal world does not always rest on narrow clear-cut principles of equality and justice; it is, rather, a web of preferences, exclusions and, contrary to what Natasha Walters once claimed, it also depends on a web of personal anecdotes. If we are not allowed to access the personal, if we think only in terms of constructs, theories and abstraction, we will be unable to benefit real lives. Hannah Arendt said it best in *Men in Dark Times*: "[E]ven in the darkest of times we have the right to expect some illumination, and that illumination may well come less from theories and concepts than from the uncertain, flickering, and often weak light that some men and women, in their lives and their works, will kindle under almost all circumstances and shed over the timespan that was given them on earth."

To this list of exclusions, preferences and personal anecdotes, the philosopher Emmanuel Levinas added the word, *love*. Love, he asserted, must always watch over what is just. I am more cynical than Levinas. His was a principle based on readings of the Old and New Testaments in order to establish conviviality between different communities, and we all know how effective that has been. I prefer to reserve my use of the word *love* to a small number of people in my personal life. Beyond the personal I would add *curiosity*, an avid interest in people's creativity and thinking beyond paradigms of authority, expertise and identity. Another word that has become quite popular is *empathy*. Perhaps the operative word in a pluralistic society should not be *love*, which remains abstract if applied to a large number of people, but *empathy*. In fact, the word is gaining acceptance as a scientifically proven phenomenon. Current scientific research indicates that the human brain carries what are called mirror neurons, multiple systems that specialize in carrying and understanding the actions of others by their intentions, the social meaning of their behaviours and emotions. The studies suggest that mirror neurons fire when a person watches the actions of another person. The mirror neurons of a person watching another person performing a task respond in the same way as if the person watching were doing the task. In other words, mirror neurons allow us to grasp the minds of others not through conceptual reasoning but through direct brain stimulation and feeling. Although direct brain stimulation can, subsequently, be mediated by thinking, its first impulse is to make the person *feel* rather than cogitate. Mirror neurons may tell us how children learn. They may tell us why a steady diet of violence is harmful or why some of us need Terminators as role models. The extent to which *the other* mirrors each of us and we mirror *the other* whose identity is not the same—including the other within each and every one of us who is not always at one with his or her own self—is a measure of the degree of freedom in which each and every one works and lives.

WORKS CITED/CONSULTED

Arendt, Hannah, *Men in Dark Times*. New York/London: Harcourt Brace Jovanovich, 1968.

Badinter, Elizabeth, *XY: On Masculine Identity*. Lydia Davis, trans. New York: Columbia UP, 1997.

Deleuze, Gilles, Guattari, Felix, *Kafka: pour une littérature mineure*. Paris: Minuit, 1975.

Derrida, Jacques, *Sovereignties in Question: The Poetics of Paul Celan*. Thomas Dutoit et al trans. Thomas Dutoit and Outi Pasanen eds. New York: Fordham UP, 2000.

_____.*Cosmopolitanism and Forgiveness*. Mark Dooley and Michael Hughes, trans. London/New York: Routledge, 2003.

———————.*Monolingualism of the Other*. Patrick Mensah, trans. Stanford: Stanford UP, 1998.

Heidegger, Martin, *Basic Writings*. David Farrell Krell, ed. New York: Harper & Row, 1976.

Levinas, Emmanuel, *God, Death and Time*. Bettina Bergo, trans. Stanford: Stanford UP, 2000.

Nancy, Jean-Luc, *The Birth to Presence*. Brian Holmes and others, trans. Stanford UP, 1993.

———————. *Being Singular Plural*. Robert D. Richardson and Anne E. O'Byrne, trans. Stanford: Stanford UP, 2000.

Steiner, George, *After Babel*. New York: Oxford UP, 1977.

Walter, Natasha, *The New Feminism*. London: Little Brown, 1998.

The Art of Alice Teichert in Three Stages

She stood at my front door carrying a large portfolio. I had never met her, nor did I understand why I should, except that the writer, bpNichol, had telephoned suggesting I meet a woman artist newly arrived in Canada whose work he thought I would appreciate. I accepted, albeit a little reluctantly, since it meant having to give up other plans I had made for that day.

After the typical, tentative preliminaries and niceties of first encounters, the woman who introduced herself as Alice Teichert opened her portfolio on the dining room table. I remember clearly the resolute way she did this, how she would not be distracted from the purpose of her visit which was to share her work.

The first few sheets of "drawings" she extracted from her portfolio took me by surprise. They seemed to be little more than carefully ink-copied texts on white paper. After four or five pages, not quite knowing how to react or what to say, I decided to look at the texts themselves for clues but the letters proved difficult to read. As I tried to read them more closely, I realized that they were, in fact, impossible to read. What I had assumed to be normal text was made up of partially formed signs, line after line of nearly-formed letters and words, each one withholding its meaning, its message, the story withheld. The structure in which language speaks had been diffused leaving in its place only traces, what Teichert referred to as *resonance*. I turned to another page. It depicted curved, vertical lines, also in black ink on white paper. It

---

* These refer to paintings dated between 1990-2000. Examples of later work can be viewed at <www.aliceteichert.com>.

was called "Silence." The next page bore similar lines, "Rivers of Space." Teichert explained that in this particular case she had taken someone else's text and traced lines between words and made their silence visible. I suddenly understood why bpNichol had assumed I would like her work. It depicted the ephemeral quality of language, the difficulty of making it say what you want, but in trying, a writer often discovers language's concrete quality while the spaces, the silences between words, take on a spatial quality. It is within this context that the Czech poet and artist Jiri Kolar's *Poems of Silence* abandon language's signifying function and rearrange letters so they no longer constitute words and phrases but work their formal and plastic aspects into graphic planes. It also reminded me of what John Cage sought to convey in his music, an activity of sounds that reveals the structure of music rather than its usual narrative lyricism.

Since our first meeting I have become more familiar with what Teichert refers to as her "text'paintings." In most, words, letters and musical notes are encrypted as tracings within boldly coloured and multi-layered paintings, while in others these notations are presented in black against white as if part of an oversized page of a book.

I have followed the development of her manuscript and published book *j'eux*, a play on words between the first pronoun singular "je" (I) and the third pronoun "eux" (they) which she turned into trialogic games between the self and others, between the three languages she speaks fluently: French, German and English, a lingual exploration of different heritages.

Heritage plays an important role throughout Teichert's work. One etymological root that recurs throughout *j'eux* comes from the Greek prefix "ana," to go back again. The writer/artist's past becomes a locus of cross-references, one language echoing another. She transposes and mutates. Nearly-formed letters and lines between missing words or between words themselves are transformed into anamorphic images different from normal reading. They give the viewer/reader new and different perspectives. Her anaphores, the repetition of words or phrases, refer to native tongues as well as to their dissolution. They open onto another creative plane, onto the artist's vision.

While Teichert manages to convey in her textual work a strong sense of experimentation and formalism, her larger canvases, on which she uses mainly acrylic paint and oil stick, summon an evocative and narrative lyricism. As the partially formed, near-visible letters of her ink drawings do not convey "realistic language," her paintings do not convey what we understand to be "realistic" images. Yet there exists in all her canvases a sense of representation which, through force of habit, the viewer seeks to confirm through the paintings' titles. However, much as the ink "drawings" elude meaning, the canvases also elude distinct imagery in spite of their titles. The paintings are not representative, yet they are not wholly abstract. They hover somewhere in between. What is being represented, at least according to the titles, is diffused through other signs similar to those of her black and white texts: ciphers, apostrophes, parentheses, curved vertical lines. As in the drawings, each painting is the product of a causal and transitive process. It encodes its own theory of reading, its own resonance, while eliciting the most lyrical responses. As in her drawings where there is constant contra-diction between languages, there exists in her canvases a contra-diction between the complexity of her expression and her resonant lyricism.

To give a few examples, within the rectangle canvas of *Invisible Helpers*, circles propagate roundness and disappear into the hard edges of the canvas. Consciousness shifts and breaks through frames in *Open Window*. In *Angels of Water*, forms swim inside luminous fluid held inside parenthetical lines. *Summer Free* is reminiscent of lines in earlier black and white drawings except, in this painting, the lines run against a luminous background.

It is evident that Teichert revels in the materiality of canvas, the fluidity and unctuousness of paint and form, qualities associated with Abstract Expressionism. The luminous quality of her work, however, sheds the opaque gravity that weighed down Expressionism for so long. As much as Teichert revels in the materiality of canvas and paint, her paintings evoke a quality beyond their surface. As the viewer steps into Teichert's parenthetical space, perception opens itself to the new, the unexpected, and the radiant.

2. Spectrum: An interview

LLT: A good place to begin is at the beginning. You were born in Paris of a Dutch mother and a German father but you grew up mostly in Brussels speaking French, German and English.

AT: And Dutch. But Dutch has receded, I don't get enough practice. I still read it, understand it, but the immediacy isn't there at this point.

LLT: Julia Kristeva, who is originally Bulgarian, lives in France, writes in French, and is also fluent in English. She has written that she lives in a polytopy, in many places at once. Do you, as a French woman from Brussels living in Canada and speaking several languages, experience this same kind of polytopic space?

AT: Very much so. Living in three or four languages has taught me to stand back from the tools I work with, not mechanical tools but living tools—because language to me is a tool that is very much alive—and having to create a relationship between these languages in order to be understood. Whatever part of this multi-dimensional space I'm in, whatever language is spoken, I tap into that dimension while being aware of the others. It's a widening experience in that I am exposed to a huge panorama that give me enough distance so that I don't have to identify with only one language. I truly believe, and I'm not saying this to try to look smart, but I feel that my true mother tongue is music. I was brought up with music and to me language is music as well. The more languages you learn, the more you realize that languages have their own melodies, their song, their swing. When you adjust to a particular swing, that language becomes fluid.

LLT: Your mother was a pianist.

AT: Yes, she was a devoted musician to the point where it took over other priorities in her life. She was a loving mother as well, but she wanted her children to learn music too. Her love of music was so strong that she used it to give us her love. For me, music is a connection to my mother.

LLT: In the eighties, there was a book of essays called *The M(other) Tongue*. The "M" was put in parenthesis to emphasize that "mother" is also "other" than the traditional mother. She is other than the object of her children's desires. You experienced, from an early age, that the mother was also a speaking subject through her music. You have two children, but because of your writing and visual art, you are obviously more than the object of your children's desires. In one of your "text'paintings" you have used the phrasing "(M)Other Tongue" but the context seems different.

AT: I was not aware of that particular book when I put the "M" in parenthesis. I came to realize that anything that has a caring effect is somehow related to certain motherhood because that is the first care we experience. When my work started to veer in different directions, I noticed there was a common line tracing its way through which would always take me somewhere else. When I started to decompose words in my writing, I experienced, as I was typing, a physical reaction, a shift. I was trying to carry my own sound through the language that I had initially learned and the end results were different from what I intended or expected.

LLT: You came to an "other" place. bpNichol once said or wrote "You trust the words to take you to what place you don't know."

AT: Exactly.

LLT: Is it also a matter of one language working against the other, a contra-diction?

AT: You have to form a unity within yourself to deal with all the languages. You have to find your note, your tune. My tune is in the "M" of music and mothering which reach out to other languages.

LLT: You have a publication coming out in France, *J'eux*. As I explained in my introduction, the title is a play-on-words between the singular pronoun *Je*—"I" in English—and the plural pronoun *eux*—"them." The book consists of games, *jeux,* between yourself and others, but also between languages.

AT: Yes. The publisher, Bernard Carlier, is also a professor at L'École des Beaux-Arts de Valence and the subject matter for one of his courses is how to publish a book digitally and via the internet, and email. As part of the curriculum, the students are using my book as their material.

LLT: This is L'École des Beaux-Arts you attended.

AT: Yes, for five years when Bernard Carlier was an assistant professor there. He was quite taken by my first text'paintings. My work was strictly graphic then but after coming to Canada three of my languages started to seep into my work and *J'eux* developed over a period of fifteen years. When I thought it was ready I contacted Bernard again. He had by then started his own publishing house, publishing experimental books, wonderful books by writers such as Jean-Luc Nancy, very current matter. I'm making a pun here, because that is what *J'eux* is all about, the current, the flow of text and language. When Bernard saw the end result, he decided to publish it.

LLT: You are effectively going back to one of your roots, one of your teachers, for publication.

AT: Yes, although he wasn't really one of my teachers, but more of a co-worker. He did have an impact, giving me pointers, directions. He could sense that I was leaning a certain way and gave me a book by Gérard Genette, *Figures 1*, because I had been talking about contemporary space, about language and space, and the conflict between spatial notation and written notation, which is also a spatial notation. There was this ambiguity between the two that I was already interested in. I read Genette, and Bernard and I would have long discussions about the semiotic and how space constitutes form. But theory was not enough for me, I needed something that was part of a reality that could be worked on physically, matter that could lead me to a beyond, to a non-physical understanding.**

LLT: Other people's theories informed the beginning of your process, but you wanted to develop your own?

AT: That's right. I apply to my work all theories useful to me because this is how you widen your panorama. But is that theory? Or the realization of something you've developed?

LLT: Perhaps it's fitting something you've developed within a theory. The belief that you are representing a certain reality, the physical or non-physical through something you've written or painted is, in itself, a theory. It depends what theory you choose to inform your work, and how you will manipulate it to make it your own.

AT: To my mind, what you are saying forms a link to music again. As a child, I had to practise intensely every day. You had to practise a lot to play well and my mind would start playing as well. When you say "it depends on the theory you choose," I'm reminded that in music there is *la clef de sol*, or *la clef de fa,* and the tone is adjusted accordingly. The rest adjusts.

LLT: Can you explain the role of music in this piece, to give the reader an idea of what we're talking about.

AT: There's a flow *un battement de mesure...*

LLT: A beat.

AT: Yes, the rhythm, *le courant.* You have the "O" which is the

---

** Within the last ten years, there has developed in France a movement called Speculative Realism. Major proponents of the movement believe that academics should work more closely with artists, not merely write about them and their work in isolated terms. Speculative Realism is distancing itself from the Kantian model that too often establishes an impassable correlation between the worlds of artistic creativity and academia. It emphasizes the importance of building platforms between different fields.

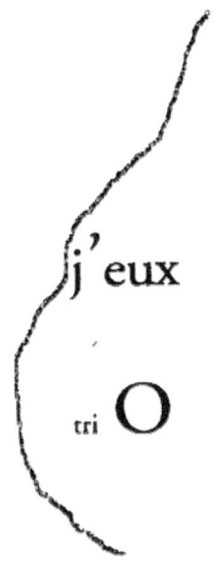

sound of singing, the "tri" of three instruments, or three languages, playing together. That is the notation, the inscription, on a spreadsheet or a score.

LLT: And the vertical line that flows between, the "river" you once called it, is the line annotating the space between the words?

AT: Yes, in music we have notes and *la barre de mesure*. I have no idea how to say this in English.

LLT: The bar, but it's more elegant in French.

AT: Yes. (Laughter) You wouldn't say "river" in music you would say "*barre,*" a straight line that organizes space. In a written text the lines between words are indications of the unspoken, a traceable space. I want to give visual pleasure. I'm reminded of Barthes's *The Pleasure of the Text*, or even Michel Butor who speaks at great length about traveling through the text. I developed a pleasure for the text, the visual dialogue within the typography—the topography—the notation. I started to play with this as I would play the piano but also improvise. I don't always play notes the way they were written but my version of them.

LLT: You were not exposed only to classical music, but also to jazz.

AT: Yes, I was trained as a classical musician and in classical ballet, but at about the age of thirteen I felt this too confining. I needed freedom of expression and I switched to jazz dance. I also wanted to learn jazz piano but my teacher didn't think it appropriate and did not permit it. He felt I was wandering too far from the line he wanted. I guess I applied it in a different way, through the visual. I discovered this through a friend of my mother's, a visual artist. How wonderfully free I felt within this domain, the making of pictures. Which were not representational at all but rather just taking a brush and tracing a line, and my expression developed in a very different way.

LLT: From then on until L'École des Beaux-Arts what kind of art were you doing?

AT: When I arrived at L'École des Beaux-Arts I'd already had two years of art studies in high school. The Lycée Berkendael in Brussels had a very complex art program. Three months before she died my mother signed my papers allowing me to transfer there. It gave me an excellent foundation in the arts. I had great history of art courses which were university calibre since the university in Brussels was teaching the same courses and we had the same resources.

LLT: Who had the most impact on you up to the time you arrived in Valence?

AT: I was leaning towards calligraphy then. Watching movies on calligraphy and seeing the brush dance, the flow. I loved scrolls, the writing of scriptures. I also looked at the intricate ways of creating images like Escher's, playing with different perspectives. But I think I was immediately drawn to writing, the application of the tool that leaves traces behind in order to communicate and convey. Well mastered, of course, like Chinese calligraphy which is known for its mastery. It's much more than a black line on paper. It swings, it radiates. I feel… *un coupe de foudre* (I am struck) every time I look at it. Calligraphy gave me the drive to explore.

LLT: So your early influences were anchored in notation or writing. You've often mentioned Dominique Fourcade in our conversations, the French art critic and poet whose writing impressed and perhaps influenced you.

AT: Yes, I came across his book *Le Ciel pas d'angle* (the sky without angles or corners), in which I discovered a panorama of everything I was interested in: song, scansion and motion, a freedom of expression. He even refers to Thelonius Monk, and quotes Cézanne: "When colour is at its richest, the form is at its fullest." All the elements I was interested in were there.

LLT: But you weren't painting or working with large canvases then.

AT: No. I was making small things but felt largeness within them. The large canvases are mainly a North American phenomenon. Well, not entirely, but...

LLT: You were more interested in "the trace."

AT: Yes, the trace that becomes the letter.

LLT: So when I look at something like *J'eux* which you call "texte'peinture" am I a reader or a viewer?

AT: I hope that you're both. I've been collecting pages from books for a long time, pages from the songbooks of Gregorian chants, for instance, where there are dots, falling lines that serve as scaffold for those dots, and words that intertwine. They are so beautiful to look at and to read. And if you look at other cultures, Sumerian signs etched in stone, Egyptian hieroglyphs, pictographs, these were meant to be read but they are all beautiful to look at. The meaning was important, of course, but how they were put into play, that's where the graphic element comes in, the layout, distributing the graphic elements into the right positions. A good composition will create vibrations within those elements and bring them to life. That's what I'm trying to work on. Perception of what is being read and viewed, their integration, and the introspection that follows.

LLT: So you are always both a reader and viewer of a book.

AT: Yes, if a book is well designed, it's beautiful to read and to look at. William Blake, for example, did both the typography and the painting in his books, but he got into trouble because he was such a deep thinker. There's an exhibition of his work in London right now, which is coming to New York, and a critic wrote in *Modern Painters* that Blake was no longer relevant to our society. He says that Blake's obsession with depth is maddening, but, on the other hand, in our present time it is insufficiently explored. It's unfortunate that Blake has become irrelevant since the exhibition is a good opportunity to introduce more depth to a superficial society. Mind you, Blake is a little too heavy for me too, but I do admire the complexity of his visual realizations.

LLT: I would like to explore your history further. You left Paris and Brussels to come to Canada. At that time you weren't doing large canvases. How did you begin to paint—what made you transfer from the page to larger canvases?

AT: I had always been interested in painting, but I didn't feel I should paint until I found my own voice in the world of painting. I did a lot of studying and I was drawn to Matisse, the great colourist. I was envious of people who could use colour and I wanted to understand why they were using it. It was a question of getting acquainted with another language again, how to use its vocabulary without fixing definitions to various colours, but rather how to apply it, make it flow, that freedom. It took me a long time. I had studied techniques of reproduction and looked at many large paintings whose artists had used printmaking, etching, line drawing, such as Matisse. So I started to use a brush on small surfaces and slowly began to feel connected to their visual expression but always in the form of inscription or a trace of a line. I saw a retrospective of Jackson Pollock which opened the door to North American painting for me and I started to do a lot of research in books and magazines. I believe it was in *Macula*, an arts periodical, that I first came across a reproduction of a Jack Bush painting, one of his line paintings, *Concerto for a Violin*, I think. A large canvas that simply depicts stripes of colour, notes, if you will, a very graphic composition. He was a graphic artist before he came to painting.

LLT: Because of your graphic background and his use of colour, Bush made an impact on you before you came to Canada?

AT: Yes. I realized I had a great affinity for colour and that I would have to leave Europe to explore North American abstract painting. Matisse had done a wonderful job... (laughter) but then I discovered paintings by Olitski, Frankenthaler, Pollock, and Rothko's orange and red squares reminded me of text blocks. It wasn't so much text as block that interested me but the flow within the texts and within the paintings.

LLT: Once installed in Canada you were very prolific. In his article on you, the art critic Ken Carpenter wrote that your work quickly achieved the look of a highly accomplished Modernist, yet he also says that the High Modernists abhor the literary in painting. How do you reconcile the two?

AT: I don't have a classic formation as a painter. I didn't get into painting by looking at nature and trying to interpret the effect that a tree has on me which is a very classic development, that's how abstraction in painting developed in some ways. I'm thinking of Mondrian who went from a tree to graphic notations of bars and primary colours on white backgrounds. I entered painting through the literary world. My text'paintings have been described as being conceptual and I've been defined as a conceptual artist, but I've never felt that way. People need explanation but I don't believe in explaining a painting.

LLT: Isn't this what we're doing now?

AT: Only generally. I like to think of the viewer entering the flow of a particular painting and becoming the maker of this object called art. If the artist has put enough in there, enough for the viewer to receive something, the object becomes more than an object. Too much of abstract art lately deals solely with technique, with the texture, as with the New New Painters. They are probably trying to stir up interest in abstraction which is an important thing to do, like the new interest in jazz. This is good because we need to stay awake to these things. However, for me, it's all very concrete, a real phenomenon, a real occurrence. For me, abstraction means thinking in terms of space, either chaotic or clear, seeping into it and, without defining too much what I mean to say, opening that space so that the abstract becomes concrete without being overly defined. Whenever I look at a painting I wonder what's beyond what is represented. I look for more than what is on the surface. I am trying to work through this in my own work. People have said to me that they don't understand what I'm painting yet they feel something. This is when I feel I've accomplished what I've set out to do. That's how I like to involve the viewer. It's an open suggestion. I hope the viewer will travel through to beyond the text or the painting.

LLT: But when you say that many painters are too concerned with technique, I think of what has now become an old McLuhan cliché, that "the medium is the message." I often find, when viewing a work of art, that the work itself is enough. I'm not sure I always want to go beyond the physical presence of a Bush painting, for example, or the fullness of a Cézanne. If the elements—colour, form—fall together, it may be enough for me. Are you saying that there should be a metaphysical aspect to all works of art, as in Blake, for example?

AT: What Marshall McLuhan was saying is very important. Our society pays a lot of attention to the medium and it's important to do so. But the medium is still a transfer of something else, something that cannot be explained, a non-physical entity that wants to be brought forth visually. In Barthe's term, the "*contre écriture*," is an energetic abstraction that carries a mystique, a secret. I want to see traces of that mysterious secret in a work of art. But we are entering an area now that cannot be defined, so...

LLT: How do you feel then when a critic creates a theory around your work that doesn't consider this non-physical entity you are describing?

AT: Well, maybe I didn't see something and the critic did. I do what I have to do and it may open doors to somebody else and I may also learn from that person. That's where the unconscious comes in. You allow yourself to seep into unfamiliar territory and get to see new discoveries later. You don't always see clearly when you're painting. Seeing is in the aftermath, in the discovery.

LLT: The process of discovery is in the articulation, like writing or speaking in an interview?

AT: Yes, exactly.

LLT: On the first floor of the Art Gallery of Ontario there's an entire wall covered with picture frames and a caption that says something to the effect that framing is decoration, a matter of taste that is socially defined. Many times when I walk into the lobby of a commercial building, for example, I find that some of our most beautiful paintings, such as a Jack Bush, have been reduced to decoration and a matter of good or bad taste. How do you feel about your paintings being used as decoration?

AT: There has to be something for everybody, but I make a distinction between painting and furniture art. Oscar Wilde said "Every art is sincere," and I can accept that but perhaps we have to define what "sincere" means. Is it to please or to explore? Is it to push the limit of the form? It's a personal choice but the work shows it. That's where transcendence comes in. No matter how objective you want to be, the work is always an extension of yourself.

LLT: As an extension of yourself, your work becomes a continuous work-in-progress and process? You're effectively working on yourself?

AT: Exactly.

LLT: Since I've met you, you have mentioned many times the death of your mother when you were eighteen. This obviously marked your art and your process. Is it possible for you to understand the extent to which she has been a presence in your work?

AT: Obviously I miss her. You are always aware of the loss but it can also be a gain. It is experienced as emptiness but it can be an emptiness that has to be filled. I couldn't listen to classical music for a long time after she died, I would start crying. So I listened mostly to jazz. I thought a lot about her, how important music was to her, the training she gave me, which was a little excessive at times because we, her children, had to do it right. This helped me develop a solid structure. She died when I was eighteen and this was a period of transition for me. I seriously started my art formation then, and although she wasn't around she was still around, maybe even more so. She helped me discover my inner tune. I don't know how conscious she was of that.

LLT: She has been a non-physical presence then.

AT: Yes, very much so.

LLT: In French, the word "spectre" can mean either ghost or spectrum as in an entire image. Listening to you, I get the feeling that your mother is a spectre in your life, not so much as ghost, but as a presence in the wider spectrum, the panorama you referred to at the beginning of this interview—the many places and languages in which you live, your *polytopy*, which has very deep roots.

AT: Yes, well, I always say that the spreadsheets of my early life are my deepest roots. It's what I always come back to. When you're dealing with matters of life and death, you better take things to heart. After her death I took almost everything to heart until I learned not to, at least not as much. But I also know that whatever I love to do, I will always have to do it right.

3. Doing It Right:
A Viewer's Response

Since our first meeting, I have often visited Teichert's various studios where we discuss, amongst other things, her work as well as art and writing in general. In the last few years, now that her children have grown and attend university, she has moved her studio away from the family home. This enables her to concentrate on her work with minimum interruption, but it also marks the boundaries with which she identifies with her role as artist, removed from other social demands and responsibilities. The studio takes up the first floor of a converted heritage building, a large expanse whose vaulted ceilings give the illusion of curved space. Shafts of light emanate from tall windows on each side of the room, while a stage at one end invites performance. It is startling to walk into this vast space where dozens of paintings lean against white walls or hang on built divisions serving as backgrounds to either finished or in-process canvases. The room vibrates, not only with colour but with creative energy. It generates its own luminosity and confirms William Blake's remark that energy is eternal delight. Teichert's studio captivates perfectly the elements of creativity I admire most: devotion and determination, and the unshakable belief that creativity matters.

As a follow-up to our first interview published in 2001, we began an email exchange in 2014, planning to go over if or how her work had changed. She answered that change is always present while the core still comes from the same place, but it is perhaps "a more anchored place between typography and painting" which still resonates throughout her work. *Resonance* remains a familiar word in Teichert's vocabulary. Her various sources or influences come from such disparate places as early book illuminations of thirteenth-century manuscripts, stained-glass windows, musical notations… all "resonate" both in her text'paintings and in her large canvases often paired as singular pieces or diptychs. The latter evoke facing pages of an open book.

As stated in the earlier interview, and not unlike many artists, Teichert often reverts to her background history when speaking of her art. She refers to when and how she learned to compose text on a letterpress during her studies in France when she was taught the importance of the space between words. It made her aware of the beauty of precision. She speaks of words as musical notes with breathing spaces on either side compelling her to read texts differently from normal reading: "A new opening to a much larger topic that I can express only visually," she writes. When I press with a clichéd question: "So you prefer to let the work speak for itself?" she answers that, of course, she hopes the work always speaks for itself. "It is about entering a state of transfer." She then adds, almost as an afterthought: "I have come to appreciate that I have no idea."

I interpret this last sentence to say that other than her background influences Teichert does not approach a canvas with preconceived ideas and I wonder if, perhaps, this was what I was trying to do in our emails. Was I trying to impose "ideas" on an artist who anchors her process in relation to what is being triggered at each step of a painting's progression? Each studio session, according to Teichert, is a unique experience that develops spontaneously. But does this process exclude ideas?

Because music has played such an important role in her background and to the development of her creativity, it is not surprising that Teichert listens to music while she paints. Both jazz and classical music lend their beat, a pulse and spacing to the tools used to apply colour to canvas or paper. She has also worked with jazz musicians, transposing her text'painting compositions into multimedia and interdisciplinary sound performances. As an additional bonus, music helps to mute the roaring and distracting sound of the ventilation fans in her studio.

It is, of course, almost impossible for an informed viewer to approach art without any preconceived ideas. It is often precisely these ideas and their development that add to art's enjoyment and edification. It helps to know what place an artist's work occupies in art's long history since no successful artist has ever stood completely alone without some knowledge of what came before, regardless how original the work may be. A knowledgeable artist carries traces of everything from art's history, from cave paintings to the most current "movement." And Teichert is an informed artist.

The purpose of this follow-up is not to explain Teichert's art, but to convey, if only to myself, how I personally react to it. Let's suppose that it is possible for a viewer to approach a painting, or an artist's entire oeuvre, without preconceived "ideas." Let's suppose the work can "speak for itself" outside the space-time of various artistic or philosophical histories or, to paraphrase the philosopher, Jean-Luc Nancy, that a painting should bring out its pure material essence which is *seeing*. According to Nancy, a work of art is not about perception or conception or meaning, but simply a mass of coloration overflowing its surface, a place where thought and ideas cross over into the simple act of seeing. When this happens it's as if the painting, or any work of art, is looking back at you. It draws you in and a deep communication takes place. I can, in fact, attest to this. It happened when I first came upon Camille Claudel's sculpture of an old woman, *Clotho*. In spite of her unseeing marble eyes, *Clotho* looked back and challenged the old woman I am becoming. Or, as another example, while I would be the first to admit I do not fully *understand* the work of Antoni Tàpies, some of his canvases move me deeply simply because they compel me to see them without trying to pin down a definite meaning. Rothko's canvases have the same effect— I see them as pure presence without representation. Teichert once said that the first time she saw a Rothko exhibition, the blocks of colour reminded her of blocks of texts. And perhaps more than any other, the work of Louise Bourgeois, especially her *Cells*, demand that they be seen without any guarantee of obvious logic or meaning. Of *Cell 1*, Bourgeois has written "I need my memories. They are my documents... If you are going to them you are wasting time. Nostalgia is not productive. If they come to you, they are the seeds for sculpture." I think of Teichert's art in a similar vein. Her memories of stained-glass windows, illuminated texts and musical notations, amongst others, are seeds that flower into new creative configurations. They are not representations but beginnings made visible, whirlwinds of brilliant colour that refer to nothing other than, perhaps, traces, seeds, and vestiges. As Bourgeois has also said, "Color is stronger than language. It's a subliminal communication." As a writer, I have found that poetry can present itself in similar ways: seeds planted in the imagination carry ideas, but they also ask that you listen for language's sonorities, its sounds divorced from meaning. As Teichert also says, "It forces you to read and hear differently."

    I should note in passing that I don't believe there are limited criteria by which to judge a work of art. Historical, philosophical, and contemporary ideas can contribute immensely to art's appreciation. If, on one hand, there is Jean-Luc Nancy's view that painting is mainly about *seeing*, there is also Marcel Duchamp's who claimed he didn't care what his paintings or his other art forms looked like, he cared only about the ideas they expressed. Both views are, to my mind, valid and in Teichert's latest work I've discovered both. Perhaps as a result of our many discussions, there are paintings I can easily translate into representations of ideas, layers upon layers of thinking. But I have also been struck by the sheer *visibility* of other works regardless of the ideas or meaning behind them. Their mere presence eclipses representation. These are the pieces that make the greatest impact on me. Perhaps also because Teichert has spoken extensively about her background including her mother's influence, as many other elements anchored in her past, I am struck by how she gives memory form. To echo Louise Bourgeois, Teichert does not go in search of memories; they are simply present in the continuum of her life and art. Creativity cannot be reduced simply to recall, but operates in the realm of the imagination where it gives memory form.

Decibel is the title of a painting and of an exhibition held at the Oeno Gallery in Bloomfield, Ontario, from August 31 to October 6, 2013. As a title it is precise and apt, the perfect introduction to a polyphonic assemblage much as a musical overture introduces different movements, arrangements and compositions to form a musical whole. Usually defined as a unit of relative loudness, its scale running between the least perceptible to ear-splitting sound, "decibel" can also refer to voltage, its current equal to ten times the common logarithm of the ratio of two readings. The painting *Decibel* can be described in all these terms. It displays itself as measures of sounds and signals. Its many layers of electrically vibrant colour give the unexpected impression of transparency. Its dominant gold colour against a dark purplish background sparkles dynamically yet it is also serenely tranquil. The predominant metallic colour bears tracings as if moving to a musical pulse. From these counterpoints there emerges at the bottom of the painting what could be pliable piano keys, tracings that can't be read for meaning, and small black squares I recognize from chant books used by students and nuns during my boarding-school days. Although most of the girls didn't know how to read these "neumes" and we simply followed the nuns' leads, we knew that they had to do with early notation of religious musical texts. It would be tempting, standing before *Decibel*, to make endless associations with religious history—small chapels, organ music, stained glass windows, psalms, hymns—but I try to stay within the confines of the canvas before me. Its presence obliterates representation. Scattered neumes capture the *essence* of sound; lines and symbols that can't be read capture the *essence* of writing; the vibrant elemental mass from which these signs emerge releases their common power, a desire to create signs and symbols in order to render the intangible visible.

The *Decibel* exhibition consisted of at least three disciplines of Teichert's work: painting, text'painting, music. Oversized double-sheets depicting alphabet letters as musical notes sat on musical stands as if the letters expected to be "played." One night during the exhibition Oeno Gallery invited a harpsichordist and flutist to give a concert of Baroque music at the gallery. Teichert's paintings surrounded the musicians and their instruments, and Teichert said it was as if her process had come full circle from her mother's influence to her own progression as an artist. She is reconciled to the fact that she is the originator of her art where her background influences—her seeds—in music, typography, painting, are moving closer together to form a whole, what I like to call a reciprocal and secular trinity. Teichert refers to the results of her process as "visual poetry" and I presume this to mean that it lays claim to an art form that resists and insists. In its finest moments, poetry resists prosaic and exhausted themes and insists on aspects other than representation such as spacing, cadence, measure, pulsation, sonority. Teichert's use of the term "visual poetry" gives her the poetic "license" to create spaces where all these elements come together.

When I decided to write a follow-up to my interview, I made a point of focusing mainly on one painting, *Decibel* since it displayed so many elements Teichert speaks of when she discusses her art. I did not, of course, ignore the other works in the exhibition, many comprising of coupled canvases, one side absorbed by deep layers of colour while its counterpart/counterpoint displayed a text'painting composition with notations, lines, neumes, traces and script. The coupling evokes different elements of an open book, a theme that always appeals to me.

Teichert and I have often discussed my aversion to certain titles that some artists give their works of art. Looking at a title before looking at the painting often prevents me from *seeing* with new eyes as if the painting's full presence had been robbed by its own representation. The title *Decibel*, however, is particularly accurate mainly because, as in music, it acts as an invitation to participate at different levels. It invites the viewer to enter a state of transfer. This was also true the first time I came upon the painting *Sans-titre* (without title), a quasi-abstract/quasi-representational painting of an open book with mostly blank pages against a vibrant background, typical of a Teichert painting. Like most of her art, it does not constitute meaning or sense as the terms normally apply to significance, but, like *Decibel*, it conveys sense as in feeling and seeing.

The large black dot superimposed on a blank page, with its facing page bearing a few red traces, reminded me of something I once read. I believe it was at a Jack Bush retrospective where he was quoted from his journals that without a period there can be no sentence. It is what Teichert refers to in French as "point à la ligne" (the period to the line). In the case of Sans Titre, the black dot emphasizes the painterly aspect of a book, the creation of its own textured/textual line.

As a multi-disciplinary artist, Teichert's creative practice branches into many areas beyond painting: book installations, book sculptures, text photography, printmaking, sound performances during which she transposes text'painting compositions vocally, often accompanied by musicians. She has recently performed with the Saskatoon Symphony Orchestra and with the Gatineau's Ensemble Prisme during the Ottawa International Chamber Music Festival. As of this writing, she is working on a new painting series, *Glyph Graph*—whose title I particularly like—and which she describes as a further reconciliation between drawing, painting, music and the printed word. It is the continuation of a project begun a dozen or so years ago after viewing illuminated texts from thirteenth- and fifteenth-century Gregorian chants. Not unlike her previous work, at least thematically, the viewer's eye is guided against a coloured background between *graphemes,* letters or symbols that represent sound, and *typography,* the appearance of printed characters on the page. According to Teichert, their alignment is a language that she senses mainly *by heart,* as it brings all the elements—painting, script, music—closer to a related whole. I haven't seen enough of this new project to comment, but as I listen to Teichert I recognize a resonance which I don't imagine will soon be exhausted. As such, I can't help but admire Teichert's dedication, her resistance and insistence as she continues to pursue what I can only describe as an alignment between thought and heart.

When a friend writes about an artist's work, there is always uncertainty as to whether the work has been seen and read accurately. Whenever I think of my thirty-plus-year friendship with Alice Teichert, during which time I followed her creative process as she followed mine, I am reminded of a quote I came across in an exhibition catalogue on Tàpies. I don't remember who wrote it and I have since misplaced the catalogue, but I jotted it down in a journal: "Artists and poets make good partners. They understand the importance of leaving traces rather than indisputable proofs."

WORKS CITED

Nancy, Jean-Luc. *Multiple Arts The Muses I*. Simon Sparks ed. Stanford: Stanford University Press, 2006.

Crone, Rainer, and Graf Schaesberg, Petrus. *Louise Bourgeois The Secret of the Cells*. New York: Prestel-Verlag, 2008.

Earlier versions of "An Introduction" and "Spectrum: An Interview" first appeared in *Open Letter*, Eleventh Series, No. 2: Summer 2001.

INTERFERENCE:
On Reading Lisa Robertson's *Nilling*

Anyone who has read Lisa Robertson is struck by her astuteness, curiosity, intelligence, and her extensive reading practice. These are particularly evident in her collection of essays, *Nilling: Prose Essays on Noise, Pornography, The Codex, Melancholy, Lucretius, Folds, Cities and Related Aporias* published by BookThug, Toronto, 2012. Her introductory essay, "Time in the Codex," states "Mostly I seek the promiscuous feeling of being alive" and a few pages further, "... I want to notice and memorize the non-semiotic meanings the codex inaugurates in my body."

In spite of the paradoxical phrase "the non-semiotic meanings the codex inaugurates in my body," it is almost impossible to read Robertson's use of the word "codex"—the collection of ancient manuscript texts in book form—without being reminded of Jacques Derrida's *Archive Fever: A Freudian Impression*. As is his usual practice Derrida offers layers of definitions as he explores the roots of "archive," *arkhē*—that which coordinates two principles in one: the principle according to nature where things begin, physically and historically, and the principle where, according to law, the social order is exercised. He examines differing principles as they apply to Freud's work and sets out to find traces of their contradictions. These are not necessarily negative contradictions in that they modulate and condition the very formation of the concept of the archive. Robertson's essays in *Nilling* also undertake a coordination of principles uniting disparate encounters. They attempt to synchronize principles according to nature where things begin, physically and historically, but also according to the social order. It is within the space of their contradiction that she introduces the concept of "nilling"—to be unwilling, or, counter-willing.

In her second essay, "Lastingness: Réage, Lucrèce, Arendt," Robertson writes that she likes to read in the early morning, preferably in bed, one of the many localities of the woman who thinks. I would question that this is a main setting for all women who think, but the image is voluptuous. Robertson writes that she thinks insofar as she reads, akin to Hannah Arendt's practice of reading and thinking. Throughout her career, Arendt immersed herself into texts and emerged from them dismantling, re-shaping and re-thinking their ideas.

If reading resists being seen, as the essay claims, and the process of thinking, as Arendt suggests throughout her writing, is an unquantifiable practice, the fact remains that Arendt's thinking about what she has read has produced, over the course of her career, more than thirty prominent and controversial books including essays, conference papers, and an extensive correspondence with a range of luminaries from various disciplines. Her reading also led to university positions as well as to editing important books for well-known publishers. She won Denmark's prestigious Sonning Prize. She considered herself an engaged citizen of the world who was unafraid of being "seen" as the instigator of controversial opinions, many of which ran contrary to traditional and philosophical ideas. In fact, she felt that too many philosophers and thinkers found participation and action in the world as distasteful, and used this as an excuse for not participating.

In Robertson's case, reading has also led to the writing of several collections of poetry, essays, university positions and academic conferences and addresses. Her writing forces me not only to think, but to get out of bed, sit at my computer and write about subjects I hadn't thought of for a while, if ever. Reading does have consequences, as Robertson's essay maintains, even if my own reading and understanding of *Nilling* may not always be accurate. Robertson's texts often give the impression of having been written from a specialist's knowledge, and in order for me to read them accurately I would have to apply a relational mode of thought which I doubt I have. It is within this context that I jot down notes as I read her essays.

"Reading... demands interference."

The title of the second essay "Lastingness: Réage, Lucrèce, Arendt" elicits a strong reaction. It is a disparate encounter of authors and I find myself resisting Arendt's and Réage's names appearing on the same page, let alone on the same line. I disliked Pauline Réage's novel, *Histoire d'O,* when I first read it several decades ago, not because of discomfort at the descriptive representation of so-called erotic pleasure due "to the embodiment of socio-moral anti-corporal values," as Robertson implies, but because it was during a period when I first became aware that "morality" depended on the freedom to choose what is moral vis-à-vis different communities instead of authoritarian social and religious laws. I was choosing to read books by women who were following in the footsteps of writers such as Simone de Beauvoir, one of the first to point out that feminine sexuality derives its chief characteristics from the fact that "woman," before being a subject to herself is an object to the other and therefore to herself. The women I was reading were re-examining and re-defining women's moral, cultural and societal roles whereas Réage's "conte" of a beautiful young woman who wants love so desperately that she accepts imprisonment, torture and annihilating rituals conveyed the usual vilification and continuance of women's historical and congenital impurity. Too many women's lives had been wasted in this brand of self-contempt and I wanted to move on.

> **Interference: How many times do we need to go over this? How many times do we have to be reminded of principles that have invariably resulted in a sado-masochistic split between what are supposedly natural and supposedly moral values?**
>
> **The thought of having to reread Réage's novel is enervating. It feels like retracing my steps backwards, re-living old battles and scripts. Robertson considers the possibility that Réage's novel is less "the signifier for genital eroticism," and more "the song of inconspicuousness, the place where will and its self-negation twist and enlace… a luminously pornographic emblem." I consider abandoning this project.**

I find Robertson's statement confusing since I believe there can be no will, or even counter-will, without the freedom to will or think. Imprisoned, Réage's character acts strictly according to the castle's law. It seems incongruous that Robertson blames people's discomfort with representations of "erotic pleasure" on socio-moral and anti-corporal values given that I can't think of any culture more obsessed with corporal values than our own. Nor have I ever read a book as less erotically pleasurable than *Story of O*. It is not, however, the main reason I find *Story of O*, or pornography and obscenity with their tiresome transgressions, "uncomfortable." I find them uncomfortable because they re-enact the same plots over and over again, exhausting themselves with the same monotonous rituals, the very antithesis of the creative imagination or the thinking mind. In a culture where more time is spent on electronic devices and less time in face-to-face encounters and relationships the questions do arise: is the problem in Western culture anti-corporal or is it anti-relationship? Is it anti-corporal or is it anti-thinking?

Interference: I was about to write that I shouldn't judge people who indulge in pornography or writers who write ad infinitum about their sex lives, but I was reminded of what Arendt wrote about "judging." It is impossible not to judge, she reiterates throughout *Responsibility and Judgment* and *Life of the Mind*, especially in the latter's appendix. Judgement, she writes, arises from a contemplative pleasure called taste and taste is inherently sociable. We tend to socialize with people who have similar "tastes." Judgement is the loom of friendship, a friendship Arendt extends to a social communicative experience, an amplification of power that no one person can have alone.

The English translation and introduction of *Histoire d'O* by Sabine d'Estrée, re-published in 2013 by Ballantine Books eBook Edition, an imprint of Random House, is prefaced by quotations from several notable contemporary sources:

The New York Times Book Review claims that the novel's "art is more persuasive than propaganda... [It aims] only to reveal, to clarify, make real to the reader those dark and repulsive practices and emotions that his better self rejects as improbable or evil..."

According to *Newsweek*, *Story of O* is a "mystical document that transcends the pornographic and the erotic... To give the body, to allow it to be ravaged, exploited and totally possessed, can be an act of consequence."

From *The New York Times*: "The publication of *Story of O*... "is an event of considerable importance. It is a significant measure of how far we have come in lifting the restrictions on art and our responses to it. In brief, *Story of O* relates the progressive willful debasement of a young and beautiful Parisian fashion photographer, O, who wants nothing more than to be a slave to her love, René."

The many pages of such testimonies makes one wonder if the

publisher feared the book wouldn't stand on its own. There's even an ambiguous comment by J.K. Rowling as if she didn't want to commit either way but neither did she want to miss an opportunity. And, in case it still escaped the reader, there's an attempt by the publisher to justify the novel's intent: it is "a warning against excessive desire," which, to me, sounds more like a marketing ploy than elucidation.

Beyond the testimonies, the reprinting of the original introduction by Jean Paulhan, Réage's real life lover for whom the novel was written, can only be described as blatant drivel in its assessment of what "Woman" is. It merely reinforces the long-held belief that "Woman" exists only as an embodiment of an idea to which she has been historically consigned and therefore doesn't exist in reality. She is but a cipher. As for Paulhan's title to his introduction, "Happiness in Slavery" one can only wonder how far removed from reality this illustrious member of *l'Académie française* really was. His unenlightened musings claiming that slaves who lived for generations under the yoke of dependence with no intrinsic self-worth are unhappy when confronted with freedom. The irony of such a statement emphasizes how Paulhan equals women's sexuality with a slavery whose only solution is to annihilate ourselves.

My reaction to my second reading of *Story of O* did not differ much from the first—it is a perfect example of sado-masochistic erosion of women's sexuality. Given that the novel may be "a warning against excessive desire," it remains and reinforces a boring genre dating back to the Marquis de Sade and beyond. The main difference, of course, is that in the case of *Story of O* self-annihilation is imagined and written by a woman. While this may present a change from the usual literary construction of the masochistic female, it is hardly progressive given she still experiences herself, according to Robertson, as "the receptacle of impurity, the gutter in whom Writing speaks." Réage's novel has also been critically described as a parody of fairy tales and of the Marquis de Sade's own novels, but given that literary parody usually ridicules a serious literary work by treating its subject matter flippantly, I fail to understand how the torture, violence, and annihilation of women in the name of love is a trivial matter. The best form of parody is one that reprises well-known texts and gives them new meaning. Much as I try, I find no new meaning in *Story of O*. Réage's book, written in the late forties and first published in 1954, was commonly compared to Sade's work whose popularity grew following WWII. It seems the more war atrocities were being exposed, the more readers looked to literature in their attempts to better understand the evil that had been inflicted on its victims. Perhaps readers could assuage their consciences by reading Sade since the torture of children and women, the satiation of unbridled appetites as described by Sade were deemed part of man's nature and strikes against the will of a disinterested God. Or perhaps what also made Sade's writing palatable to the intelligentsia was how his torturous episodes were invariably followed by intellectual discourse. As Sade became more presentable and respectable in his stance against morality and God, the inclination to aestheticize evil grew.

Interference: I refuse an invitation to attend the presentation of the baroque opera: *The Infernal Comedy: Confessions of a Serial Killer* **starring John Malkovich who portrays the charismatic criminal, Jack Unterweger, who hoodwinked an entire nation—Austria—into believing his innocence. "Sentenced to life imprisonment for murdering a teenage girl, Jack Unterweger reinvented himself as a literary celebrity in his acclaimed autobiography,** *Purgatory*. **Hailed by the country's intellectual elite as a triumph of rehabilitation, he was paroled in 1990, only to claim the lives of 11 more women on two continents." The reviews describe the manipulative portrayal by Malkovich,**

accompanied by the music of the Vienna Academy Orchestra in arias by Haydn, Mozart, Vivaldi, as brilliant. Portraying evil in literature, on stage or in films—especially if it is backed by intellectual exposition or classical music—is easier to portray than humdrum non-evil, and certainly more lucrative. Tickets to *The Infernal Comedy* sold out within a few days.

Robertson refers to *Story of O* as "banal" and I agree. I find the story "banal" as Hannah Arendt defines the word in *The Origins of Totalitarianism* and in *Eichmann in Jerusalem: A Report on the Banality of Evil*. Arendt has been severely criticized for using this widely misinterpreted phrase and perhaps it is necessary to be reminded that Arendt did not consider Eichmann's activities during the war trite or banal, far from it. She meant that *the factors* for which people are willing to betray themselves and others are often insignificant because they are without *thought,* without *will,* without *judgement* as in Eichmann's case. In such circumstances evil possesses neither depth nor any demonic dimension. It simply continues to spread like an unchecked fungus over what should be our most basic human values.

As daring and bold as *Story of O* purports to be, it is worthy to note that Réage felt it necessary to hide her true identity as its author for at least 40 years. Although the book was first published in 1954, Réage only publicly revealed herself to be its author in an interview in *The New Yorker* in August 1994. Pauline Réage was the pseudonym of Anne Desclos, who felt it necessary to use yet another pseudonym, Dominique Aury, when she worked as an editor and a translator at Gallimard, one of Europe's most prestigious publishing houses. Desclos also publicly admitted in a television interview two years before her death in 1996 that she had written the book to spice up her affair with Paulhan, her long-time married lover, because a) he had claimed that women couldn't write pornographic novels, and b) she felt she was getting too much competition from younger women. She was forty-seven years old when she wrote her novel, and Paulhan, chief editor at Gallimard, was a well-known womanizer of seventy. It was primarily for these reasons that both felt it best to keep her identity secret.

Interference: December 17, 2012. A twenty-three-year-old woman, a paramedical student from Delhi, boarded a bus with a male friend on their way home from a movie. When the bus deviated from its route and the woman's friend became suspicious and objected, the six men on board started to taunt the couple, especially the young woman. When her friend tried to intervene he was beaten, gagged and knocked unconscious with an iron rod. The six men then raped the woman.

Battered and bleeding, the young woman and her friend were dumped near an expressway. Authorities did not release the name of the rape victim as it is considered shameful to have been raped in India. Several pseudonyms are being used by various media outlets: *Jagruti* (awareness); *Amana* (treasure); *Nirbhawa* (fearless one); *Damini* (lightning). Most protesters refer to her as "Damini," from a 1993 Bollywood film whose lead female character fights for a victim of sexual assault. A non-fictitious woman who was gang-raped and thrown off a bus is given a fictional name from a Bollywood movie because it would be too shameful to use her real name.

Interference: Medical reports suggest that the woman who was gang-raped in Delhi suffered serious injuries to her abdomen, intestines and genitals. The doctors believe a blunt object, suspected to be the iron rod used to beat up her male friend may have also been used for vaginal penetration. The rod is described by police as a rusted, L-shaped implement of the typed used as a wheel jack handle. According to a police spokesman

> the youngest of the six men was the most brutal. He sexually abused his victim twice and ripped out her intestines with his bare hands.

I am not about to argue that pornography does not titillate. As Robertson's essay points out, Réage's text may represent a contemporary and simplified view of Epicureanism as a commitment to sensual and erotic pleasure, but, as she also points out, Réage's text is not, in fact, an accurate view of Epicureanism. While Epicurus lauded the gratification of natural desires, he drew a clear distinction between natural desires and artificially cultivated ones. One of his principal doctrines is the virtue of *justice,* originating in a pledge of *mutual* advantage to restrain men and women from harming one another. His quasi-cult following insisted on three requirements: equanimity, bodily health and comfort, and a life of moderation and prudence. Sado-masochism and self-annihilation hardly live up to mutual advantage, comfort, moderation and prudence, but it is quite possible that in present-day culture, misreading past texts are irrelevant since contemporary and popular views rely either on selective memory or no memory at all.

What often passes as culture nowadays is entertainment in which viewers are given the *illusion* of interacting with reality. This is most evident in the popularity of reality TV shows with their insipid narratives, video games with their constructions of masculinity rooted in an iconography of power, violence, and seduction around gender-coded narratives. Entertainment often consists of avatars ruled by technology, spatial navigation, triangulation and, most importantly, the commercially viable. Taste in the arts is, more often than not, defined by what is generally communicable by representation without the mediation of perception or thought. It would seem we have reached Hannah Arendt's future as described in *Between Past and Future* (published in 1961) in which she explores cultural history from ancient times to what she foresees as its future when cultural values are replaced by ephemeral entertainment. It would seem we are becoming nations of avatars and the future has arrived.

Interference: The more I read about Damini, the more I feel suffocated by the brutality of the event. I want to respond but I don't know how. It is as if I had been misplaced within someone else's order and put out of action.

On Dec 19, 2012, Damini underwent her fifth surgery, removing most of her remaining intestines. By December 25 she remained intubated, on life support and running a 103º fever due to severe sepsis. On December 27 she was flown from a hospital in India to Elizabeth Hospital in Singapore, a multi-organ transplant speciality hospital. Some reports suggest that the decision to fly her out of India was made when it was clear that she would not survive the next 48 hours. Damini died on December 29, 2012.

Thousands of women and men throughout India gather to protest against Indian rape laws, but the police respond with water cannons, tear gas and sticks. Speaking out against the protesters, the president's son, Abhijit Mukherjee, refers to the protesters as heavily made-up women who have little connection with "ground realities." Asara Bapu, spiritual guru, blames the victim because she did not "chant God's name and did not fall at the feet of her attackers." One of the suspect's lawyers, Nabigar Kak Sharma, says his client is not guilty of the charges because an unmarried couple should not have been using public transportation or walking the streets at 9:30 p.m.

The main accused, Ram Singh, driver of the bus, who refused to undergo an identification test in court boasts he tortured and raped the girl to teach her a lesson after she bit one of her attackers in self-defense and because she also tried to prevent them from assaulting her friend. Witnesses say he tried to run her over after throwing her off the bus. Ground realities indeed.

On one hand, an academic initiative by the Arab Studies Institute is critical of these reports for fear they are being exploited by "Orientalists" to promote racist stereotypes. On the other hand, many activists are proud that India is leading the way for the world in efforts to address violence against women.

Badri Singh Pandey, Damini's father, restores her true name: Jyoti Singh Pandey. He wants the world to be a witness to what was previously deemed unrepresentable and save his daughter's honour.

In her book-length study, *Colette*, Julia Kristeva examines the many variants of Eros created by Colette via her characters' relationships with men, women, beasts, even plants, all of whom metamorphose into the act of writing. While pornography remains a narrow domain that keeps perpetrating the same means to the same ends, thereby suffocating new ideas, feminine pleasure in Colette's novels is continuously re-defined through the act of writing. Between the real and the imagined, there is the place of the word. According to Kristeva, Colette found a language to express an extraordinary osmosis between sensation, desire, anxiety, and the infiniteness of the entire world:

> In fact Colette's writing is not focused on the organs, even less on the sexual organs. For her all the senses are sexual organs, differing from our ordinary perception only in the respect that, at the very instant she experiences the elements, the elements also experience her: loving/loved, subject/object… The barriers among the five senses, lithe threshold between intimate perception and external reality that lies behind them, are posited only to be transcended. They are catwalks, never boundaries.

Kristeva also issues a caveat: "After reading Colette, you're left with a sense of self-evidence that the usual literary criteria fail to capture. " Indeed many critics have failed to grasp the sensory sense of Colette's texts. If they did, they found feminine sensuality as it relates to the act of writing so unimportant as to dismiss it, unlike Réage's novel which set off waves of *frissons* throughout the French publishing world when it first appeared. In fact, it did so again upon the publication of Angie David's biography *Dominique Aury* by Éditions Léo Scheer in 2006.

As Robertson points out, the reader who identifies with Réage's "allegory" in order to authenticate the psychological impetus of the narrative is subjected to a highly uncomfortable twisting. "And," Robertson writes, "I do identify, in part because I can't resist her sentences... Each sentence unspools to a filmic plenum. But it is more than her style that causes my absorption. She represents in surreal detail the humiliation of bearing the trope of femininity, as my own body has in other ways naturalized that trope."

How old, I wonder, does one have to be to disengage from this persistent "trope"? When will we give ourselves permission to decipher *who* we are instead of relying on symbols of a servile will? For several decades women with whom I have developed a "loom of friendship" have stopped experiencing femininity as humiliation. Most, if not all—professor, writer, artist, film director and film buff, editor, stay-at-home mother—refuse to metaphorically reconcile their fates to degradation in spite of what is being presented nightly on television, in films, books, newspapers. Metaphors and tropes are too often used to defuse the dehumanization of human beings instead of giving rise to autonomous thought. The language of the servile will inevitably degenerates into a language of defilement.

Interference: Three young women who had been missing from nine to eleven years were found in a house in Cleveland, Ohio, where they had been kept prisoners by their captor. Throughout their ordeal they had been bound by ropes, chained or padlocked in a basement or in bedrooms. They were raped, beaten, tortured.

Between Robertson's sections on *Story of O* and Lucretius's *De rerum Natura*, Robertson introduces Hannah Arendt's *The Life of the Mind* made up of two books: "Thinking" and "Willing." The third section, "Judging" was not completed before Arendt's death although the subject comes up throughout *The Life of the Mind* and the posthumous publication, *Responsibility and Judgment*.

The dozens of colorful tabs affixed to the pages of my copy of *The Life of the Mind* indicate I have returned to this book many times over the years. Whenever I do I never fail to witness a life fully lived, fully thought out. If one follows the span of her publications, from her thesis on St. Augustine as a young student to the last chapter of *The Life of the Mind*, one will notice a maturation, a slight shift in her assessments, an indication of an ever-developing mind.

In the "Willing" section of *The Life of the Mind*, Arendt explores how Hegelian "Will" draws upon the past for its ideas and images creating an antagonistic relationship with "Thinking" as experienced in the "now." She explores "Willing" as an attempt to build a bridge between the Willing ego and the Thinking ego, between "What" and "Who" a person is. "What" a person is, according to Arendt, is invariably reduced to social and biological attributes whose definitions are often anchored in the past. A person's qualities, gifts, talents, and shortcomings may make her unique, but those particularities reflect "what" she is in the sense of a specimen that loses herself in the anonymity of the species. "Who" a person is, on the other hand, is the separate being that appears clearly and unmistakably to others. Although this *who* acts in the space of appearance, she does not treat herself as mere concept or object nor is she defined by social or cultural utilitarianism. *Who* she is, as Kristeva suggests in her book *Hannah Arendt*, is disclosed in an action distinguished from collective acts, an action as source of creativity projected toward both past and future.

As different as Colette's and Arendt's writings are, the exploration of their writing leaves a reader with a sense of self-evidence vastly different from a text such as Réage's. Metaphors, as Arendt points out in *The Life of the Mind*, are not meant to stay solely within the mental realm. Living beings are as they appear but they are not mere appearances. They are in the world and not merely of it:

> Analogies, metaphors, and emblems are the threads by which the mind holds on to the world even when, absentmindedly, it has lost direct contact with it, and they guarantee the unity of human experience. Moreover, in the thinking process itself they serve as models to give us our bearings lest we stagger blindly among experiences that our bodily senses with their relative certainty of knowledge `cannot guide us through.
>
> ...[L]anguage, the only medium in which the invisible can become manifest in a world of appearances, is by no means as adequate... as our senses for their business of coping with the perceptible world... Metaphors therefore can be used by speculative reason...but when they intrude, as is their tendency...they are used and misused to create and provide plausible evidence for theories that are actually mere hypotheses that have to be proved or disproved by facts.

To Arendt's description of metaphors as hypotheses, I would add tropes used for rhetorical effect such as humiliation as trope of femininity, or, at the other end of the spectrum, goddess as trope of love. As Colette and Arendt point out, femininity does not confine itself to one body, to either mother or sex object, or slave or goddess, but constitutes itself as a unique *who* within the plurality of the world in which her many "bodies" participate.

Although Arendt felt at home in the world, she often referred to herself as a "foreign girl." Fully engaged in human diversity, she sought to retain her uniqueness and live out her singularity of "who" she was even if it meant she didn't always fit in. This is wonderfully exemplified by a light and amusing anecdote in Elizabeth Young-Bruehl's biography, *Hannah Arendt: For Love of the World*. Arendt had befriended the poet and novelist, Hermann Broch, an inveterate ladies' man who spoke openly about his conquests. Arendt admired Broch's writing and while his private life did not shock her—she was not easily shocked—the embarrassing situations Broch often caused his friends and lovers puzzled her. When he attempted to include her in his retinue of female seductions and made a pass, Arendt's response startled him. Unlike other women who made themselves readily available, primarily because he was a well-respected writer, he discovered that Arendt not only found him resistible, she was able to decline his advances with delicacy: "Hermann," she said, "let me be the exception."

Interference: Let me be the exception.

Hannah Arendt was a woman who presented new ways of thinking. She would be the first to admit she was not always "right" on every assessment or stance; no one ever is. Her thinking process shifted as it evolved over the years. The passion with which she explored "her taste and judgment," however, did make her an exception. Her boundless need to understand and to commit her explorations in writing was part of her process of discovering *who* she was. She strove to think in a pluralistic way depending on realistic circumstances rather than on social, cultural or idealized conditioning. Without ignoring the past and its philosophers, poets and novelists, her personal and political experience directed her to the present-day world. While living in mutual reliance with other thinkers she strove to think for herself. In word and deed, she inserted herself into the paradoxical plurality of unique human beings. Thinking prepared her to meet whatever she had to in her daily life, a kind of midwifery that left her empty at times so that she could re-think her position without resorting to dogmatic rules or guidelines.

Robertson ends her essay by quoting part of Lucretius's poem, *De Rerum Natura*. While the essay moves away from a reading of annihilation in Réage's text with its endless desire, expectations, seductions, dependence, and passes briefly through Arendt's extraordinary thought processes, it ends on a simple note, a feeling of love.

I agree with Robertson that the quoted excerpt of Lucretius's poem is beautiful. It addresses Gaius Memmius, member of a powerful Roman senatorial family. It implies friendship, fellowship, love, and the sharing of ideals amongst followers of Epicureanism, an autocratic group who devoted a fair amount of time to the attempted conversion of non-members in spite of its free-will philosophy. Lucretius was the first writer to introduce Roman readers to Epicureanism and considered Epicurus an infallible master, the moral and spiritual saviour of humanity much as a devotee of any cultish figure. Vanquished by the never-ending wound of love, the inspiration of poetic productivity, Lucretius's poem sheds light on the physical world while Epicurus brings light to the spiritual world.

Many writers, from Ovid to Montaigne, from Rimbaud to Lautréamont, have used the symbol of the clinamen that Robertson's essay refers to—a deviation, a swerve from a hail of atoms thrown into the vacuum along parallel trajectories. Simone de Beauvoir used it. So did Harold Bloom to describe the inclination of some writers to "swerve" from the influence of predecessors. Marx and Engels regarded Epicurus and Lucretius as major thinkers and the theory of the "clinamen" one of the sources of their dialectics. Scientists, including Darwin, and researchers of the chaos theory, agreed that *De Rerum Natura* with its rainfalls of particles tumbling into a void with some of them swerving from their trajectory was not too far from scientific truth. The term has also been used extensively by modern and postmodern theorists such as Gilles Deleuze, Jacques Lacan, Jacques Derrida and Jean-Luc Nancy.

The vacuum in which atoms travel and tumble in a downward direction into an endless, bottomless abyss is a powerful metaphor; according to Lucretius, a body cannot extract itself from this law of gravity even if some manage to deviate from it. It may illustrate much of our physical and material world, the precariousness of our lives, but it leaves out one of the most important elements as it applies to human beings: consciousness. Consciousness cannot be reduced to a sum of particles. By her own example, Arendt's "Let me be the exception," has shown that in a thinking world, women and men are more complex than swerving particles or the twists and turns of clinamina. In a thinking, willing and judging world, men and women are capable of re-thinking themselves as each one experiences *who* she or he is. Who wrote that materialism is the philosophy of the subject who forgets to take account of *who* he is? I can't remember but it does sound apt.

The readability of a poem varies according to the divergence between the social code by which a poem was written and a reading that no longer conforms to that particular social code. As lovely as Lucretius's didactic poem on nature is, the variance between codes of the past and codes of the present is so broad that I feel mainly distance from ethics based on the past ills of an imperial society. I feel distance from a poet who traced the cause of evil to pagan gods while I trace it to non-thinking men and women trapped within inflexible codes. If we apply this atomistic theory to human beings devoid of consciousness, how will we judge those who swerve from the norm regardless of whether they do good or bad in this world?

I am not clear how Robertson defines "moral will" or "natural impulses." It seems, however, that if both men and women do not re-think the definitions of these terms, we will fail to think *who* we are in our own time and towards our own future. Perhaps it is between the juxtaposition of women's annihilation of the self, as in *Story of O,* and an image of idealized love, as in Lucretius's poem, *De Rerum Natura,* that Robertson's essay creates a space of "nilling" in which to make conscious choices. Perhaps it is through this realization that Robertson can end her essay with: *I feel love.* I assume that this feeling includes a love of the self.

At one point during her career Arendt had planned to write a book titled, *Amor Mundi* (Love of the World), until she recognized that love was best reserved to the private sphere of family and a few close friends. Outside this immediate circle Arendt thought all human beings should be treated with respect as each one of us would want to be treated, as she suggests in *The Human Condition*:

> Yet what love is in its own narrowly circumscribed sphere, respect is in the larger domain of human affairs. Respect... is a kind of "friendship" without intimacy and without closeness; it is regard for the person from the distance which the space of the world puts between us.... Thus the modern loss of respect, or rather the conviction that respect is due only where we admire or esteem, constitutes a clear symptom of the increasing depersonalization of public and social life.

Interference: What did Jyoti Singh Pandrey feel between December 17, 2012, the night she was attacked and raped and

the day she died from her injuries on December 29, 2012?

What did Amanda Berry, Gina DeJesus and Michelle Knight feel while imprisoned, tortured and abused for ten and more years in that house of horrors in Cleveland Ohio? Did they, at any time, have the opportunity or freedom to swerve from their captor's will? Did they experience the room where they were held as the place where will and its self-negation twist and interlace?

What about the hundreds of young girls in Nigeria kidnapped from their schools by Boko Haram?

What could the young aboriginal woman, Loretta Saunders, have been thinking moments before she was murdered and her body dumped in a ditch along the Trans-Canada Highway?

Twelve-year-old Rehtaeh Parsons?

Tina Fontaine?

Rinelle Harper?

Brandy Vittrekwa?

The twelve hundred First Nations women who have disappeared?

......

I can't imagine what any of these girls and women might have thought or felt but I doubt it had anything to do with love or respect.

WORKS CITED

Arendt, Hannah. *The Life of the Mind.* New York: Harcourt, 1971.
_____ *The Origins of Totalitarianism.* New York : Harcourt, 1966.
_____ *The Human Condition.* Chicago: University of Chicago Press, 1958.
_____ *Between Past and Future.* New York : Viking Press, 1968.
_____ *Eichmann in Jerusalem.* New York : Penguin Books, 1994.
_____ *Responsibility and Judgment.* New York : Schocken Books, 2003.

David, Angie. D*ominique Aury*. Paris: Editions Leo Scheer, 2006.
Derrida, Jacques. *Archive Fever A Freudian Impression.* Trans. Eric Prenowitz. Chicago: University of Chicago Press, 1996.
Kristeva, Julia. *Colette.* Columbia University Press, 2004.
_____ *Hannah Arendt.* Columbia University Press, 2001.
Réage, Pauline. *Story of O.* ebook, Ballantyne Random House, 2013.
Robertson, Lisa. *Nilling.* Toronto: Bookthug, 2013.
Young-Bruehl, Elizabeth. *Hannah Arendt, For Love of the World.* Yale University Press, 1982.
_____ *Why Arendt Matters.* New Haven: Yale University Press, 2006.

Uncceremonial Bodies:
Nanni Moretti's *We Have a Pope*, Margarethe von Trotta's *Vision*, Robert Lepage's *Le Confessional*.

I: Nanni Moretti's *We Have a Pope*

Because I spent my childhood in Catholic convents, it is perhaps not surprising that I am fascinated by films featuring nonconformist religious themes. During the viewing of Stephen Frears's *Philomena* whose story often takes place in a convent I whispered to my husband: "Those are exactly like the dormitories and iron beds I slept in as a girl." The ambience and cultural setting of the film brought back a flood of memories and reminded me why films as Nanni Moretti's *We Have a Pope*, Margarethe von Trotta's *Vision*, and Robert Lepage's *The Confessional*, amongst many others, were so compelling.

Around the time when the Catholic Church was casting about for a new pope following the abdication of Pope Benedict, I rented the Italian film *Habemus Papam—We Have a Pope*. So many aspects touched on issues that have frustrated me over the years—conformity, various psychoanalytical theories, political and religious totalitarianism. It did also touch, however, on key interests—individualism, non-conformity and the dominant role that representation plays in our society.

The opening scenes of *We Have a Pope* depict rituals following the death of a Pontiff. Black-clad nuns mime prayers at the defunct's coffin, undoubtedly praying for his soul; one-hundred-

and-eight red-cassocked cardinals robotically chanting "*ora pro nobis*"—pray for us—file into the Sistine Chapel, transformed into a voting room; a throng waits in St. Peter's Square for the black or white smoke that will announce whether or not a new pope has been elected. During the voting process the cardinals behave like cheating schoolboys taking exams in study hall as they try to sneak a look at their neighbours' voting sheets. Those who have been identified as the most likely candidates silently pray: "Not me, Lord, I'm not up to it." On the third vote, Cardinal Melville, played by the legendary Michel Piccoli, is selected. I assume the choice of the surname "Melville" by the director was no accident. Many parallels can be drawn between Moretti's film and Herman Melville's novel, *Moby-Dick*. The main characters of the movie and the novel are metaphorical instruments rather than rounded characters. They live according to some impersonal force and are, for the most part, lost to the outside world. It is difficult not to draw parallels between the male-bonding of Moretti's cardinals and Melville's sailors, especially the scene where the sailors extract spermaceti from a dead whale. Perhaps the most obvious analogy is between some of the cardinals and Ahab's "hubris," the flaw which leads superheroes to defy common sense in their belief that they are immune to the laws of nature.

Following the appearance of white smoke indicating the election of a new pope, the Vatican balcony doors open onto St. Peter's Square to the cheering of the crowd below. As the new Pontiff is being introduced, a scream is heard from behind the curtains. It is an invisible but audible scream, reminiscent of several paintings depicting screams such as Edvard Munch's or, more precisely, Francis Bacon's studies of *Velásquez's Portrait of Pope Innocent X* depicting a purple-caped figure sitting on a papal throne, his mouth frozen in a shriek.

"I can't do this," the Pope-elect Melville declares as he walks away from the balcony with his baffled attendants scurrying behind him. The situation is without precedent and there is no guide to direct them as to how they should behave. After a physical examination determines that nothing physical is amiss with the Pope-elect it is decided that another kind of specialist should be consulted: a professor psychoanalyst.

The role of the professor psychoanalyst is superbly played by Nanni Moretti himself. His initial demeanour of being fully in charge is soon decimated by the conclave's dogmatic rules. He is reminded by one of the leading cardinals that the soul and the subconscious cannot co-exist. He is, therefore, not allowed to broach subjects such as family background, dreams, fantasies, sexuality or crisis of faith; plus the meeting will take place before the entire conclave of cardinals. Unable to make any headway under such circumstances, the professor psychoanalyst refers Melville to his estranged wife who is also a psychoanalyst and whose office is in Rome, outside the Vatican walls, in the real world. She and the professor psychoanalyst are estranged mainly because they are so competitive in their professional lives, especially since she seems to be more successful than her husband. Her specialty and success revolve around identifying "parental deficit" problems in her clients' backgrounds. It doesn't take much imagination to make the leap from "parental deficit" to Freudian concepts of parental-child relationships such as the Oedipus complex. The scene highlights how Freudian concepts rely on the application of theories much as religion does. They both seek to explain the invisible through "signs." They both depend on the Word—religion through confession and psychoanalysis through disclosure, a kind of secular confession—in order to give events meaning. The analogy is not so farfetched since the word "psychology" was created in the fifteenth century by Christian theologians engaged in the study of the human soul, an invisible entity separate from the body. In a succinct formulation of Christian orthodoxy the function of the soul for man was to act as God's viceroy. By the end of the nineteenth century, Freud, as he worked to build a more scientific basis to his analytical method, replaced the soul with the mind in his attempt to discover "signs" that would serve as the basis for his methodology.

When the woman psychoanalyst, unaware of the Pope-elect's true identity, asks about his profession, he replies that he is an actor. As a child and young adult he had dreamed of becoming an actor but was rejected by a theatrical company in favour of his sister so he settled for a role in the clergy instead, a stand-in for God. He became a character in a religious theatrical production.

As he leaves the psychoanalyst's office, Melville is able to elude his entourage and break free. Overwhelmed by the outside world he takes refuge in a department store, the secular church of consumerism and commodity. When he appears overly anxious and explains to a helpful young woman that he suffers from "parental deficit," it is likely that he is referring to a power higher than his earthly parents and he now feels abandoned.

Time weighs heavy on the cardinals who are not allowed to leave the Vatican until the Pope-elect returns and is properly introduced to the throng still gathered outside. To while away the time the professor psychoanalyst creates volleyball teams pitting cardinals of different countries against each other. Although the Pontiff is not in his apartments, every "sign" that he might be is met with anticipation—the fluttering of curtains, music heard from his apartment, a stand-in who voraciously consumes the meals meant for the Pope-elect. Whenever the stand-in walks by the windows and creates a shadow of the Divine Representative, he is cheered and adored. Who needs the real thing when absence and ceremonial representatives reinforce the cohesion of belief?

As Melville manoeuvres his way through the city, he is consistently exposed to acts of kindness. He meets up with a theatrical group who, not unlike the Vatican, offers community and devotion, and is headed by a slightly unhinged director. On a bus, Melvillle reflects on the crumbling of St. Peter's Church and I was reminded of a line from my French Catholic convent days: *Tu es Pierre et sur cette pierre je batirai mon église.* (Because of the name "Pierre" which means "stone," the pronouncement works better in French than in English.) As more of these large stone buildings serve increasingly smaller congregations and can no longer be maintained they are either demolished or used for purposes other than religious rituals, such as upscale condos or theatres. The conversion of names—Pierre and Peter—also remind me of The Peter Principle: what works initially is used in progressively more challenging situations until it reaches its own level of incompetence then fails. It seems nothing is set in stone in perpetuity and all rituals will eventually abolish meaning.

It is not that Melville is losing his faith, but that he is no longer seduced by the accumulation of representational symbols that surround it. In creating dogma and requiring subjects to subscribe to it unquestionably, by establishing it as the theological and moralistic order upheld by a compliant candidate makes the pope an arbitrary ruler. It is a role that the Pope-elect Melville cannot, in all conscience, accept. He returns to the Vatican with an altered message for the expectant throng still gathered in St. Peter's Square: In order for the Church to survive it must embrace change; it must find new ways of thinking for it has petrified just as Peter the Rock has petrified and, consequently, the entire Catholic population. What is needed is a new kind of Pope who is capable of effecting this change. Melville recognizes that he is not that person. A Pope must represent not only dogma, he must also be his own *dramatis personae*, a role Melville is unable to assume. He is at peace with his decision but, once again, the conclave of cardinals is devastated. Entrenched in their rules and ways of thinking they cannot see that perhaps Melville's decision, based on a pope's infallibility, may also be God's will.

When the present Pope Francis was elected, people kept referring to the event as "a sign" that Catholicism was about to make significant changes toward a more progressive church. Pope Francis's consistent choice of a simple white cassock instead of the more elaborate papal robes, his eschewing the usual luxurious apartment and pope-mobile, proved promising for people whose faith is reinforced by symbols, miracles, or "signs." There are, however, "signs" that there is little room for change within the Catholic Church even under such a pope as Pope Francis. In his message prior to the 2014 Soccer World Cup in Brazil, Pope Francis recommended that the games be a showcase for teamwork and solidarity, a need for respect and honour, which seems reasonable enough. Unfortunately, he followed this with "To win we must overcome individualism…" It may be good advice where commercialized sports are concerned; however, one gets the feeling that Pope Francis's recommendation was meant to reach beyond the world of sports. Any culture or religion that cannot accommodate individualism or independent thinking remains in the grip of absolutist thinking.

II: Margarethe von Trotta's *Vision*

Margarethe von Trotta's recent film, *Hannah Arendt*, focuses on a four-year period in Hannah Arendt's life during which she attended the Eichmann trial on an assignment for *The New Yorker*. It emphasizes one of the most important themes running throughout Von Trotta's cinematic work: breaking through socially imposed limitations and what it means to think differently. Arendt's post-trial report, as all her writing, speaks of the importance of resistance. Arendt is portrayed as being actively engaged in defining original ways of thinking instead of simply returning to the old order before World War II. It emphasizes the importance for individuals to question the consequences of traditional thinking versus the fundamental characteristic of each individual's thought process.

For her film, *Vision*, Von Trotta explores her trademark theme of resistance, this time through the mindset of a twelfth-century nun, Hildegard von Bingen. It is set at a time when most women were illiterate except for those belonging to the aristocracy or for those who were placed in convents by their parents as was the case with Von Bingen. They might have done so because she suffered from mysterious seizures. From the age of eight she was raised in a monastery according to the founder Saint Benedict's ascetic rules overseen by Benedictine monks. Later, as the Abbess, Von Bingen refused to perpetuate traditions as defined by the monastery's style of worship and penance such as self-flagellation and the wearing of barbed-wire corsets. If God gave women bodies, she reasoned, He didn't intend them to mistreat them to the point of throwing them away. "He who kills the flesh kills the soul that inhabits it" she reflects in the film. An avid reader, she overlooked forbidden laws such as reading in the garden. She cultivated plants and herbs for medical purposes. She was convinced that music soothes and therefore heals, and performed her own compositions including her then famous musical morality play *Ordo Virtutum*. When she encountered too much opposition from within the monastery, mainly from the Benedictine monks and especially from their Abbott, she took her causes to the Archbishop, and even to the Pope. When one of the young nuns, pregnant by one of the resident monks, was labelled a seductress by the Abbott, Von Bingen insisted and obtained permission to build a monastery away from the monks. She was a reformer who believed in science. Unlike so many religious fanatics who, supposedly, devote their entire lives to God, she cared deeply for human beings. In fact, most of the women in Von Trotta's films believe in absolute love towards others, the reason perhaps they are often so lonely in such matters. Even so, Von Trotta's heroines have few complexes about being strong women. It is interesting to note that in *Hannah Arendt*, Arendt's great love was Heinrich Blücher, an innovative political thinker, and not the philosopher, Martin Heidegger, as so many Arendt biographers would want us to believe. While Arendt did have a relationship with Heidegger while she was a student and he was a professor, she became highly critical of Heidegger's political and philosophical views, as demonstrated in many of her writings, including her magnum opus, *Life of the Mind*. She was well aware how some philosophers, including Heidegger, fabricated and adhered to concepts that intrinsically interfered with creative thinking.

While Von Trotta began her career as an actress, her first solo directional debut *The Second Awakening of Christa Klages* in 1977 introduced what would become constant themes in her later work including the complexities of female bonding. She followed this debut with *Sister or the Balance of Happiness* about two sisters whose emotional and symbiotic relationship makes it difficult to live independent lives leading to one sister's suicide. The movie was well received except for a critic at the *Chicago Tribune* who complained that it was too serious. She then directed *Marianne and Julianne* also known as *The German Sisters* in 1981, a worldwide success, followed by *Sheer Madness* in 1982. This was followed by the extraordinary *Rosa Luxemburg*.

In *Women and Film: Both Sides of the Camera*, Ann Kaplan points out that certain women directors, such as Marguerite Duras, Agnes Varda and Claudia Weill, provide new idealized images of strong and beautiful women who do not depend on the male gaze. Considering the period during which they were made, these directors' films were innovative and are to be admired, but Von Trotta's characters face more complex and difficult struggles in their attempts to define *who* they are in situations where the dominant discourse—be it male or female—continually undermines their efforts. Their struggles are, more often than not, alienating, lonely, dangerous or downright suicidal. There are no happy endings. One only needs to remember Rosa Luxemburg's face, as portrayed by Barbara Sukowa, as she turns for a last look at the love of her life, Leo Jogiches, played by Daniel Olbrychski, as she is led away after being arrested. They know they will never see each other again. One of the most interesting elements of this biographical film is how Von Trotta delves into every aspect of Luxemburg's private life from an early age through adulthood in order to show how it influenced and established her political views. From a young age, Luxemburg had a clear vision—perhaps too clear—of a path she believed could lead to a more peaceful and just world. As a small girl, Von Bingen is repeatedly told by her surrogate "mother" nun that her heart will be revealed only to some.

Oliver Sacks, author of *The Man Who Mistook His Wife for a Hat*, raises the possibility that Hildegard von Bingen might have suffered from migrainous and/or epileptic seizures. Apparently the two are often connected. During such seizures, he describes how the subject suddenly experiences herself as being outside this world but still aware of what is going on around her. He reproduces some of Von Bingen's drawings of what she experienced during these seizures: backgrounds formed of shimmering stars set upon wavering concentric lines; showers of brilliant stars extinguished as they fall into an ocean; stars turning into black coals falling into an abyss; figures radiating from a brilliantly luminous central point. The remarkable consequence of Von Bingen's seizures is how she turned them to her advantage and presented them as coming directly from a higher power. She referred to the Bible to explain how her seizures were meant to change certain rules established by human beings, mainly the monks who resided in the same monastery. Considering how little was known about seizures and their causes in the twelfth century, Von Bingen may well have believed they came from God, but she also saw them as opportunities to advance non-conformist views to improve the nuns' living conditions. Her seizures became encounters with a brain that no longer functioned robotically. In fact, it rejected a pre-ordained system that prevented its devotees from acquiring authentic and original knowledge. As Sacks points out, hers was "a privileged consciousness, the substrate of a supreme ecstatic inspiration. One must go to Dostoievski, who experienced on occasion ecstatic epileptic auras to which he attached momentous significance, to find an adequate historical parallel."

In his study of cinema, Gilles Deleuze developed an original view of the mind that refuses to function by preset plans and clichés. He proposes a brain where new paths, new connections and ways of thinking and seeing are established, a proposal which is gaining credibility in scientific circles as more and more evidence points to the brain's ability to change itself, what is referred to as the brain's plasticity. Von Bingen's "visions" remind us of many artists and writers whose works challenge preset thinking. There are endless examples of this throughout the history of art and literature, of artists and writers who produced works that did not communicate in traditional ways, but whose main objectives were to create new paths towards new thinking as Von Bingen's visions and revisions did for her.

From her first films dealing with sisters there has been ample criticism regarding the plausibility of how sisters are paired in Von Trotta's films, each one of whom is, in one way or another, a double of the other. As Kaplan points out, this doubling is not a mere externalization of an inner split, but the strong attraction that certain women feel for qualities in other women that they themselves do not have. "Sometimes, the doubling takes place on the imaginary/symbolic axis, one of the pair functioning smoothly in the public sphere, while the other sister seems to desire regression to the presymbolic..." In other words, not all women are the same or share the same values. I find the question of "plausibility" vis-à-vis the imaginary/symbolic axis bewildering. Is the purpose of art meant to reflect everyday plausibility? The strength of Von Trotta's art is not merely to project reality but to travel to its other side in order to reach the imaginary. Von Trotta's heroines consistently face disappointment, weariness and loss, but they also imagine and dream. Those dreams represent the reasons why they are drawn to lives of resistance in political, religious or social spheres. Each woman's journey is challenging but also less compromising of personal values. For those of us who are mere spectators to such imagination, it makes everyday reality infinitely more rewarding.

The last scene shows Von Bingen riding away from the cloistered community of nuns with Brother Volmar, her staunchest supporter. When she first confessed to him that she had visions and heard voices he replied that she must heed the voice, reveal that which is hidden. He recognized that the articulation of her visions was pure poetry. The *Decretum* established by the first Ecumenical Council in the mid-twelfth century, a document that states the principles of church law, specifies that any violation of those laws would render the violator a lifelong wanderer. As a talented and original thinker with gifts Von Bingen believed could only be bestowed on her by God, she could no longer adhere to laws established and maintained by a dogmatic and resentful hierarchy. Faced with constant opposition from those in positions of power, she leaves the monastery she built with the help of her "sisters" and for the remaining years of her life she intends to use her talents to communicate directly to the people at large.

The reviews of this film when it was first released were, for the most part, perplexing. A few reviewers described it as "feminist," presumably because creative and independent thinking women are considered "feminists," whereas I've never heard of creative and independent thinking men referred to as "masculinists." A few reviews also branded the film as "lesbian-ish" on the assumption that "sisters" who live in cloistered circumstances and have only each other for emotional support must be lesbians. In spite of the fact that Von Bingen states very clearly that she considers one of the young nuns who acknowledges her works as "daughter, mother, sister." When a rare and unlikely renewable source of acknowledgement is taken away from her, Von Bingen becomes frantic, somewhat hysterical. It would seem that, not unlike Freud, many reviewers believe there can be no psychology without sexuality, not even when it comes to mothers, daughters, and sisters, an unfortunate assumption that perpetuates a locker-room mentality.

III: Robert Lepage's *Le Confessional*

> Lepage makes spectators the real subjects of his journey of discovery, not his film's characters...—Aleksandar Dundjerovic

There are few more edifying experiences than encountering a book, a painting or sculpture, a play or film, that challenges one's way of seeing and thinking. The choreography of Pina Bausch for example—how her dancers' gestures can't always be explained yet they *make sense* in the way they *touch*. You walk away from Bausch's choreography wanting to hold on to that feeling before getting caught up in the usual cycle of "but what does it mean?" In the same vein, some movies—fewer and fewer, I'm afraid—leave you riveted to your seat after the lights have come up, aware you have witnessed creativity that stands apart from the crowded field of cultural production and representation.

The Italian film, *The Great Beauty*, is such a film. It opens with a tourist taking photographs of Rome's extraordinary archeology and historical sites. In the midst of recording his visual memories, a choir singing ecclesiastical music in the background, the tourist is suddenly struck dead. For viewers, also mere tourists in life's game of sightseeing, there can only be one ending. The scene is immediately followed by a predictable response to death, diversions in the form of a loud, drunken party celebrating the main character's sixty-fifth birthday. Jep, flâneur, cynic, world-weary narrator, is a dissipated one-time novelist who now writes articles for a newspaper on pointless and socially fuelled art performances. It is an unfortunate occupation since Jep's perceptive voice-overs and monologues are reminders of human frailty, and of the crassness of much of what is new and without history versus the beauty of what is memorable. Against this realization, and the words of a century-old nun—"Roots are important"—Jep comes to the realization that a writer, or any successful creative mind, builds on memory and bridges past to present in order to produce meaningful work. In Jep's case, it may lead to a second novel.

Robert Lepage is very adept at creating such bridges. As symbols of passage, they allow his protagonists to cross different time frames and various cultural and linguistic settings including exchanges between his creative and personal life. His first film, *Le Confessional*, dedicated to his father, is Lepage's acknowledgement of his multi-linguistic and cultural roots. His French-speaking birth parents adopted three English-speaking children and Lepage remembers family conversations conducted in two languages. In fact, Lepage's entire oeuvre's reason for being is to connect disparate identities, cultures, languages in order to reach beyond boundaries and borders. From the beginning of his career he wrote in Canada's two official languages. One of the most spectacular examples was a co-direction with Gordon McCall of Shakespeare's *Romeo and Juliet*, in which McCall directed the Romeo/Montague passages in English, while Lepage was responsible for the Juliette/Capulet scenes played in French, a perfect metaphor for the French/English situation in Canada. The play was well received in Saskatoon, Stratford, Ottawa, Toronto and Sudbury, but it never played in the province of Québec. As Lepage has pointed out in interviews, in Québec the play would probably have been considered too federalist. *The Dragon's Trilogy* also played to packed houses for a month in London England in spite of the play being two-thirds French. Robert Lepage is one of the first Canadian playwrights, perhaps the only one, to suggest that as a nation, we should no longer be threatened by the "other." His first film, *Le Confessional*, as all his work, operates around the idea of duality: two brothers, two periods, two languages, two bridges that connect Québec City.

The early period during which *Le Confessional* is set was a time of significant cultural shift in Québec's religious and social boundaries. As Aleksandar Dundjerovic points out, "Québec is... culturally and nationally unstable terrain, made of a set of social contracts where the need to preserve the past collides with a pragmatic present..." *Le Confessional* uses flashbacks of its past—Québec's motto is, after all, *Je me souviens*—in order to trace and better understand Québec's potential for reaching out beyond its borders. It also underlines how memory is depicted through the creative representation of powerful images.

The film opens with a voice-over: "*Le passé porte le présent comme un enfant sur ses épaules.*" The past carries the present like a child on its shoulders. The main character, Pierre Lamontagne, has returned to Québec from China to attend his father's funeral. A generation has passed. The son's given name, Pierre, "stone," coupled with Lamontagne, "the mountain," recalls once again the phrase conveyed to the apostle Peter, "*Ton nom est Pierre, et sur cette pierre je batirai mon église.*" Lepage uses the name Pierre Lamontagne in much of his cinematography and theatre, a persona on which he sets out to build, not a church, but the foundation of a journey of discovery, bridging where he came from to where each creative project leads him.

The missing father is a recurring theme in Lepage's work. Even when a birth father is present he has little impact. "What am I supposed to do with a grade-four education?" Lamontagne's father asks his wife, Françoise, Pierre's mother. It is a reminder of a time when the role of the birth father was diminished by and subordinated to an overly authoritative and symbolic representation of fatherhood when priests and the church-backed Premier Maurice Duplessis played dominant roles throughout Québec's culture.

Lepage's use of flashbacks of Hitchcock's film *I Confess* contrasts two periods, one before the Quiet Revolution and thirty years later when the Church no longer holds an authoritative position as exemplified by the film's defrocked priest, Massicotte, who subsequently becomes an overbearing politician. It is nevertheless Massicotte who holds the last piece to the Lamontagne family's secret: the real identity of Pierre's adopted brother, Marc, information the defrocked priest uses to blackmail Marc into having a homosexual relationship. The history of sexual abuse by priests and the harmful implications of the secrets of the confessional to which priests are sworn are not lost in flashbacks of either Hitchcock's or Lepage's films. It is also significant that Lepage's multi-disciplinary company, Ex Machina, founded in 1994, omitted from its name the "Deus" that usually accompanies the original phrase "Deus ex machina," god from the machinery. In Greek theatre, gods were either suspended above the stage or waiting in the wings to intervene when mere mortals were incapable of solving their dilemmas. Lepage prefers the creative and collaborative machinery of the members of his company with which to experiment and develop new ideas.

The concept of confession is not used only in a religious sense throughout Lepage's work, but also as metaphor for acknowledging what was once culturally surreptitious and disgraceful. Pierre sees Marc's nude body in a gay bathhouse through a grille reminiscent of the grille between confessor priest and penitent, the first time he becomes aware of his brother's sexuality. He later learns that his brother is, in fact, bisexual, blending once again categories. Lepage often uses partitions such as the confessional box, phone booths, shoji screens, film screens, etc... to suggest divisions between cultural and time frames.

It is impossible not to connect Marc's name to the outlines of a crucifix, religious icons, and photographs of family members on the walls of the apartment where the family once lived. These marks show through like ghosts, and prove impossible to eradicate no matter how many coats of red paint Pierre applies to the walls. The colour red plays an important role throughout *Le Confessional*: blood in a bathtub signals the end of a pregnancy, as it also signals Mark's suicide, also carried out in a bathtub; occasional flashes of ecclesiastical red are reminders of a history shaped by subordination, power and violence. Pierre is only successful in covering the outlines when he uses the colour blue, symbol of cleansing. There is no need to linger over the *mark*s left by good or bad memories. Robert Lepage, via Pierre Lamontagne, moves from the passive metaphor of imprints and simple recall to an active and creative imagination.

The aim of this short essay is not to analyze the plots of Lepage's film, or Moretti's and Von Trotta's, but to emphasize the importance of creative thinking in the making of art, regardless of form. In all three films, memory—mother of all Muses—can only take place by becoming an image through the present representation of an absent thing. It is the main factor in building bridges from the past to the present and, consequently, toward the future. The last scene of *Le Confessional* is of Pierre Lamontagne carrying Marc's young son on his shoulders as they cross a bridge. He is at peace with the past and assumes the responsibility of carrying on his shoulders a human being, Marc's child. What awaits Lamontagne and his nephew at the other end of the bridge is the consequence of that crossing, of thinking creatively in order to change aspects of a culture held for too long in the grips of inflexible, symbolic, political and religious control.

All three films question narrative identities: human beings prove more important than exhausted rituals and symbols; memory that simply repeats bears all the *marks* of *habit*; memory that simply repeats is opposed to memory that imagines.

To paraphrase Socrates's dictum that a good life is a life worth telling, I would add that a good life is worth sharing if it is a life fashioned by creative thinking. While each individual must acknowledge the social facts of the community in which she or he lives whether it is religious, ancestral or cultural, each one should recognize the existential validity of creative thinking within those communities. Sister Hildegard's view that God did not give women bodies so they could merely be thrown away could also apply to each individual's imagination.

WORKS CITED

Dundjerovic, Aleksandar. *The Cinema of Robert Lepage: the poetic of memory*. London: Wallflower Press, 2003.

Kaplan, E.Ann. *Women & Film*. New York and London: Menthuen, Inc., 1983.

Sacks, Oliver. *The Man Who Mistook His Wife for a Hat: and Other Clinical Tales*. New York: Touchstone, 1985. 166-172.

Richard Serra and Kim Ondaatje:
A Matter of Time

My definition of site-specific art may be unduly flexible since I seem to find it everywhere. Or, at least the potential for site-specific configurations, the ability of forms to reconfigure space as it intersects with different genres: performance art, video installations, landscape, architecture, sculptural projects, parks, neon signs and, to use a theoretical term, the semiotics of urbanism. I became aware of this potential the first time I saw the prairie sculptor Joe Fafard's installation of seven bronze cows on a small piece of grass in front of the Toronto-Dominion Centre in Toronto's financial district. The building consists of two tall, black, slick towers designed by Mies van der Rohe, master of urban design. I will leave it to the reader's imagination how those seven cows, resting as if in a prairie pasture reconfigure space in an otherwise sterile financial district. It was around the same time that I came upon a light-emitting diode flashing a Jenny Holzer truism along a section of Yonge Street in downtown Toronto. The section featured, and still does, strip joints and sex clubs where an eleven-year-old boy had been recently abducted, molested and murdered. Holzer's diode read, *"What urge will save us now that sex won't."* Her truisms are often intentionally banal, and serve to expose the perverse banality present in much of the urban scene where so much revolves around youth, appearances and forged representations of sexuality and reality. By simply walking through this strip of Yonge Street I felt like a participant in its sordid setting.

There are so many sites and site-specific artists one could write about: Maya Lin's monument in Washington commemorating the fifty-eight-thousand American casualties of the Vietnam War. The site, carved by a long, black and highly reflective wall, draws attention to a nation's conscience during a precarious moment in its history. It reminded me of Robert Smithson's mirror displacement pieces such as *Mirror Shore: Sanibel Island*. I've only seen it on film, but you can still experience how water and mirrors reflect one another much as Maya Lin's monument where the names of the dead and the reflection of the viewers mirror each other. One of the main differences, of course, is Maya Lin's monument is meant to stay in place for a long time, whereas the mirrors in Smithson's displacement pieces are removed or his earthworks such as *Spiral Jetty* are re-absorbed into nature.

There are of course Christo's reconfigurations of landmarks in wrapped buildings, bridges and various sections of parks and landscapes. There is the enigmatic Joseph Beuys who planted seven thousand oak trees in Kassel to show how live trees change the landscape as they grow over time. Speaking of time, I don't find site-specific art only in contemporary, post-modern installations. I found it in the Sicilian and Roman columns of temples several thousand years old, their massive skeletal profiles abstracted from their original forms. They create iconic and ironic exchanges between past, present and future as they reconfigure topographies while works originally conceived as site-specific pieces are being rescued by museums and stored away in an attempt to preserve them. And sometimes the obvious comes from the mouths of babes as when I took my grandchildren to the Toronto Reference Library one afternoon. We were on the fourth or fifth floor, looking down the centre well to the first floor, when one of them exclaimed, "Wow, look at all that space!" If it hadn't been for the curved ramps framing the well, he would never have seen "all that space."

More and more, buildings are being designed so they do not serve merely as functional storehouses but instruments of the creative spirit, of observation and knowledge. Museums are being conceived and built to fit particular sites as Frank Gehry's Guggenheim Museum in Bilbao, Spain. Its design is an extraordinary combination of interconnecting shapes integrating the city's urban buildings against the backdrop of the Nervion River and surrounding hills. Orthogonal blocks of limestone contrast with sinuous forms covered in titanium where gulls catch their reflections as they fly by and become living components of the building. Curvilinear shapes challenge standard architectural right angles. Glass curtain walls add light and transparency to an already light-infused space. In short, the building completely reconfigures the 32,500 square meter site and its surroundings and the traditional idea of what a museum should look like.

When you enter the museum you are confronted with an array of site-specific pieces that have either been commissioned for the museum or retrieved from original sites. There is much to take in but what immediately stands out are the various components of Richard Serra's installation *The Matter of Time*. The massive steel pieces mould the space they occupy, their size and presence overpowering but also inviting. *Snake*, for example, three massive sheets of steel comprised of identical sections inverted into each other, form narrow and curving pathways. As soon as you enter one and make your way between the steel sheets, you feel their weight, their industrial texture interfacing with the cultural atmosphere of the museum. You experience claustrophobia, disorientation, awe, but also the sensation that you have been invited to be a player in the continuum of an original work of art.

After several hours visiting the various rooms of the museum several people outside join others who are walking in and out and through the legs of an enormous sculpture of a spider by Louise

Bourgeois. Here too we are players in the continuum of a sculptural field, walking through the legs of a piece titled *Maman*.

In his book, *Artists' Gardens*, Bill Law writes that breaking boundaries is a lonely business and it is not surprising that so many artists choose to retire from previous lives, from controversy, and retreat into the private worlds of their gardens. Such is the case with Kim Ondaatje.

It's not that Ondaatje is a recluse. On the contrary, a visitor could easily be overwhelmed by the constant stopover traffic at Blueroof Farm in the Lake District north of Kingston, Ontario. And the comings and goings are not only of people. For years various animals have competed for space and attention at Blueroof—cattle, dogs, cats, geese, ducks, deer, frogs, and at least one bear. One of my favorite stories—and there are many—involves a goose by the name of Bruce, a long-time resident at Blueroof. One morning, while visiting, I heard knocking at the front door and when I answered a goose making a terrible racket marched imperiously into the living room. "Kim" I shouted, "there's a goose in the house and he is very upset." "Oh, that's Bruce," Kim answered nonchalantly. "The dogs must have been teasing him and Lily again." Apparently, whenever the Dalmatians, which Kim bred for thirty-six years, "teased" Bruce or his mate, Lily, running circles around them, Bruce would knock on the door with his beak and tattle on them. There are so many such stories. I recently received photographs Kim had taken of a dozen or more deer on her front lawn because they know they will get fed there during long harsh winters when their natural food source grows scarce.

Before Ondaatje moved from Toronto to Blueroof Farm on a permanent basis in the early eighties, she was already recognized as an important Canadian artist, photographer and filmmaker. From her early paintings of the fifties and sixties, including *Sumac* and the *Hill* series, it became apparent that landforms occupied an important place in her imagination. She has often spoken of how the *Sanctuary* series arose, in part, from reflections while on solitary canoe journeys. The metaphorical seeds which would grow into life-long relevance were not only sown early, they were carefully nurtured until Ondaatje created a sense of space so personal and intimate that it became impossible to separate it from her very core. As Lora Senechal Carney points out via a quote by Gaston Bachelard in the catalogue *Kim Ondaatje,* "Space that has been seized upon by the imagination cannot remain indifferent space, subject to the measures and estimates of the surveyor." The catalogue was published on the occasion of a retrospective exhibition which travelled from Museum London in 2013, to The Robert McLaughlin Gallery, Oshawa, in 2014, to the Agnes Etherington Art Centre, Kingston, in 2014-2015.

Even as a committed environmentalist, Ondaatje found beauty in Canadian industrial sites, which led to the painting of her *Factory* series in the 1970s. While many critics and curators have emphasized the political aspects of this series, Ondaatje has maintained that it was not meant to be political:

> I do not care for either art or gardens with a message. My industrial landscapes, for example, aren't anti-pollution paintings. When I did them I was simply intrigued by these geometrical shapes, the mystery of not knowing what goes on inside them and the beautiful movements of smoke or steam dispersing into the air and creating a misty atmosphere around the factory.

This is not to imply that Kim Ondaatje is not political. Again, anyone who has visited Blueroof Farm will have heard her views on the devastation of the environment. It was partially because she could no longer justify pouring caustic materials down her drains that she gave up painting. But it is not a subject she incorporates into her art. Instead, the *Factory* series draws the eye to the subliminal communications of soft colours dotted with dark geometric forms against hazy and snowy backgrounds. It is easy for a Canadian who has lived in the northern clime of industrial Ontario to relate to these, not so much for nostalgic reasons but as grounding in the experience of place. Her series, *The House on Piccadilly Street*, has a similar effect. *Sideboard with Lamp*, for example, uses the reflective surface of a mirror to project content into the viewer's space, thereby enclosing the viewer in the experience.

At Blueroof Farm, near Bellrock, Ontario, Ondaatje has spent the last forty years cultivating a seven-acre garden carved out of the Canadian Shield she refers to as her "final canvas."

Walking through Ondaatje's "final canvas," her "tame wild garden," as she calls it, is as exhilarating, if not more, as exploring any other serious art form. A canvas will, more often than not, insist on interpretation, on content, versus form. The lilies, chrysanthemums, hostas, ferns, various grasses, bulrushes, bright orange tulips flanking boulders of moss-covered bedrock, trees of various shades and height, gazebo, a bridge reminiscent of Monet's spanning his famous water lily pond… leave little room for interpretation. There is no need to draw a line between content and form. It cannot be said "this is not a garden" as Magritte once claimed of his famous painting *This Is Not a Pipe*. Blueroof's overflowing scene touches all senses: the gaze lingers; the humus-scented air pervades; velvety lilies picked for the dinner table leave their traces on clothes, fingers, a cheek; the produce from the organic vegetable garden cannot be matched by any store-bought counterpart.

When I visited Blueroof Farm in the fall of 2014, parts of Ondaatje's "final canvas" had begun to concede their place to the elements. This was partly because it was fall when such a process happens naturally, but it was also because of Ondaatje's age. She is no longer able to maintain the garden to the extent she once did, nor can she afford to have someone else do so. As Ondaatje has pointed out "...if the lawns are not cut, the beds weeded and edged, the trees and shrubs trimmed, my garden could return to the wilderness within a year. Goldenrod, burdocks, chicory, bugloss, dandelions and hosts of other so-called weeds would take over and it would be a wilderness again. Nothing is forever." But it also takes more than age to overcome Ondaatje's indomitable spirit. One of the first things she announced when I arrived for my visit was that she had planted, the day before, one hundred tulip bulbs and she still had another eighty to go. She is not quite ready to relinquish her final canvas.

It may seem incongruous to compare Ondaatje's and Serra's art. Although Ondaatje is only ten years older than Serra, her interests and creativity seem to stem from an earlier time than his. Still, there are many similarities: their university studies were both steeped in literature; they were both influenced by American Transcendentalism; they both decided early in their careers not to work in the then dominant language of Abstract Expressionism; they both developed an interest in gardens; both have worked extensively with photography and film, one genre often informing the other. And, as Serra has pointed out: "People start making art... because they're interested in an alternative way of living, of using their own time to reflect on their own experience." There is no doubt Kim Ondaatje deliberately chose her alternative way of living.

Both Richard Serra and Kim Ondaatje gave up painting to explore the concept of three-dimensional space outside the contained field of the painted canvas. It was upon seeing Velázquez's *Las Meninas* that Richard Serra was able to write, "I realized there was a split between the interior illusion of space and the projected space I was standing in and that I was the subject of the painting and Velázquez was looking at me... I was the subject of the painting... The painting forces you to self-consciously participate in its reflection by including you, the viewer, on an equal footing within its space... My initial steps into the reality of three-dimensional space had begun, and my painting days were definitely over." It was around this time, in the mid-sixties, that he purportedly threw his completed canvases into the Arno River and started to think in terms of viewers becoming part of his art. It was also around this time that he juxtaposed stuffed animals with live animals in cages to emphasize the difference between illusion and reality.

Most, perhaps all, of Richard Serra's sculptures, such as the eight pieces that make up *The Matter of Time*, interface either with the cultural atmosphere of museums or with large expanses of land. Most, if not all, give the impression they are intransient and will not succumb to the elements any time soon. They may be, as their name suggests, *The Matter of Time*, but the pieces also imply that time is infinite. Not so the living garden at Blueroof Farm where the garden will return to its natural order well before Serra's. "Nothing is forever," Ondaatje has said, and it is perhaps befitting that many of the trees, bushes and flowers she planted are dedicated to the memory of writers and artists who once visited her Blueroof Farm. It is impossible to make one's way through this memorial trail, often accompanied by cats and dogs, even a few cows on some occasions, without feeling you are a participant in its reality and in its continuation as long as it is part of Blueroof Farm. In challenging notions of the work of art as a static object, Ondaatje opens up each participant's perceptual field. In walking through and seeing, sometimes touching, or taking in the scent of evening primrose, the divisions between artist and viewer, between object and subject are obliterated. All who pass through and contribute to the creation of this memorial trail become a player in its time:

On the strolling path around Orser Pond,
trees and shrubs planted in memory of writers
and artists who visited Blueroof Farm, flourish
in spite of bedrock:

a tamarack grove for Greg Curnoe
a golden willow for Matt Cohen

a weeping cypress for Roy Kiyooka
a weeping willow for Roy Kiyooka

a weeping elm for Al Purdy

white pine for Kathleen Milne

English oak for F.R. Scott
a silver spruce for Marian Dale Scott

lilacs for Bronwyn Wallace
Japanese cherries for Gwendolyn MacEwen

a lilac walk for Jack Chambers
a white birch for Olga

on the edge of the pasture, forming a corner,
two maple rows for Tom Marshall

at the top of the laneway
and near the milkweed monarch garden
sumac for beep,
    sumac,
       sumac,

and one golden locust

The question I want to ask: if I* were to have
a tree overlooking Orser Pond what would it be?
What rock-bird would nest in my arms?
Enter the sound aspiring to the rustling of leaves.

The pronoun "I" can be replaced by the reader's name.

Shortly after this poem was published in *Site-Specific Poems* (Mercury Press, 2004) Kim phoned to say she had planted a Blue Spruce tree dedicated to me at the top of the laneway. The only living person to have a tree, she added. It was only a few inches tall when planted and I have kept track of its growth on visits to Blueroof. When I saw it in the fall of 2014 it had grown a good four feet and was completely surrounded by bpNichol's sumac gone wild and autumn red. I try not to make too much of this...

BOOKS CITED
Hobbs, Robert. *Robert Smithson: A Restrospective View.* Dusseldorf:
 Wilhelm Lehmbruck Museum, undated.
Serra Richard. *The Matter of Time*, Bilbao: Steidl Publishers, 2005.
Laws, Bill. *Artists' Gardens*, United Kingdom: Ward Lock, 1999.
Getty and Townsend, *Kim Ondaatje*, London: Museum London, 2013.
Tostevin, Lemire Lola. *Site-Specific Poems.* Toronto: Mercury Press, 2004.

What's in a Name?

I was asked to write about my origins as a writer. As a child, I entertained ideas of becoming many things—nurse, teacher, writer, actress—the latter having something to do with my name. My mother, as a young woman, had determined to name her first daughter "Lola" after some actress she'd heard of by the name of Lola Montez. Because it was such an unusual name in the small Francophone community in which we lived, the explanation was repeated many times. As my mother learned more about Lola Montez's notorious background, she would invariably follow the story with a laugh and add, "My daughter was named after a dancer who couldn't dance." To this day, whenever I get writer's block, I paraphrase: "I'm a writer who can't write" and am reminded of the advice Alfred Hitchcock gave Ingrid Bergman when she complained that she was not feeling the character she was playing on a particular day. "Well," Hitchcock apparently replied, "fake it, my dear. Fake it."

Other than the Montez story, I first heard my name in the 1959 American version of *The Blue Angel*, a remake of the original Von Sternberg film starring Marlene Dietrich. The American version wasn't very good but it did alert me to the German version. I had heard it was a classic and I eventually viewed it at a cinematheque in the sixties or seventies. It was my impression that Dietrich's character was given the double moniker, Lola-Lola, to emphasize the violence and cruelty of the vamp she portrayed. It wouldn't be the only time my name would be associated with such intrinsic worth. Think of the Lola character in Céline's *Voyage au bout de la nuit* encouraging men to become war heroes thereby leading them to their deaths. She represents the quest for dreams that betray ordinary reality.

Nabokov's novel *Lolita* differs substantially from the film. In the novel, the twelve-year-old is always referred to as "Lola" by everyone except for Humbert Humbert who has given her his own pet nickname "Lolita" meaning little Lola. It is a strategy to deny Lola her full subjectivity as the novel follows, from Humbert's perspective, his obsession with pre-pubescent girls. The movie, however, omits Humbert's history and Lolita is portrayed as an older fourteen-year-old seductive nymphet, in a kind of Lolita syndrome that sexualizes young girls and does not allow them to live out their childhoods. Hollywood's switch from Nabokov's uncompromising and disturbing insights into a middle-aged man's aberrant obsessions to sensational and titillating pabulum taught me, for the first time but, alas, not the last, the difference between art as exploration and exhibitionism parading as art.

While my ambitions of becoming an actress waned, I maintained a lively interest in films, but a greater one in literature. Through movies and books I learned the role of self-invention, how easily the self can be reduced to a sign and how easily this sign determines who you are in the eyes of viewers or readers. Marguerite Duras's *The Ravishing of Lol Stein* fascinated me mainly because the novel is based on a memory of Lol, the "a" of her name missing indicating the characterization is not complete since it is based on absence. Jacques Demy's film title, *Lola*, masterpiece of the French New Wave, is a stage pseudonym for a dancer whose real name is Cécile. Shot in the sixties, the plot and the characters' destinies rely on missed opportunities and anticipate Tom Tykwer's *Run Lola Run* where every character's fate also depends on chance. Franka Potente who plays the title role is portrayed in the opening credits as a larger-than-life cartoon character, a kind of de-facement of both the character and the real-life person.

Fassbinder's *Lola* stars the incredible actress, Barbara Sukowa. She plays a singer in a brothel whose real name is Marie-Louise. Sukowa recently appeared in Margarethe von Trotta's *Hannah Arendt* a film based on an episode in Arendt's life. While the film didn't have any characters bearing the Lola name, Sukowa did win a Lola, the German Oscar, for her portrayal of Arendt, one of my personal heroes.

In a holiday apartment my husband and I once rented I discovered a collection of stories for children written by a grandmother, Lola Basyang, an alias I later discovered of Severino Reyes, the Filipino writer. It is a refreshing reversal from when women used male pseudonyms in order to have their writings published.

In June 2014, in the "Summer Reads" section of *The Globe and Mail*, I came across a review of Charles Foran's novel, *Planet Lolita*. I haven't read it, but the review states that it is set in a near-future Hong Kong and tells the story, in the dialect of social media, of Sara Kwok, a fifteen-year-old upper-middle-class girl who has a brush with the sex-work culture of the city. The main theme of the book, according to the review, is the sexualisation of young Asian girls, the inhabitants of "Planet Lolita." It would seem that novels set in the future, told largely in the dialect of present-day social media, can't shake their reference to the sexualized monikers of the past.

Do all these references to my name *sound* inordinately narcissistic? I suppose they would if they were based on a consistent, unchanging reality of a self instead of the imaginary's ability to create an ongoing and changeable chain of doublings as in films and as in writing. Or if my story of how I became a writer was constituted of a discourse that "I" completely master. Alas, not unlike the character, Lola, in Ian McEwen's *Atonement*, I am a casualty whose destiny depends mainly on misrepresentation.

Asking a writer to write about her origins is akin to asking an actor to explain how the many characters she has played correspond to who she is. It reduces the diffusion and complexity of different roles to a self-absorbed confinement. Realism in literature is nothing more than its own imitation.

So, please believe me when I write that I may be the Devil's assistant in the Broadway musical, *Damn Yankees*, where Lola always gets what Lola wants. Or perhaps I am the transvestite in a song by The Kinks and I walk like a woman but talk like a man. Am I Barry Manilow's showgirl? Or perhaps I began to write simply because I liked the idea of my name appearing on book covers.

Writers are fictional characters of their own making. They expand the imagination and give writers and readers access to a world of appearances in order to explore the many sides of human beings in relation to an unpredictable, diverse and ever-changing world. Our fictional selves are our true birth certificates.

ACKOWLEDGEMENTS:

"A Touch of Evil in Carsairs" first appeared in *Alice Munro: Reminiscence, Interpretation, Adaptation and Comparison*, Buchholtz and Sojka, eds. Peter Lang Publishing Group, Frankfurt, Germany, 2015.

"A Difficult Place to Stand: a review," appeared in *Canadian Poetry*, No. 71. Fall/Winter, 2012.

"The Burning Alphabet" was presented at Influency: A Toronto Poetry Salon, overseen by Margaret Christakos, spring, 2007.

An early version of "New Configurations for an Old Alphabet" appeared in *Open Letter*, Eleventh Series, No. 7: Spring 2003.

"Letter to a Friend" first appeared in *Canadian Fiction Magazine* No. 66, 1989.

An early version of "Mistaken Identity" was given as a plenary talk at the annual meeting of the Association of Canadian and Québec Literatures, UWO, in 2004, and appeared in *Open Letter*, Thirteenth Series, No. 3: Summer 2007.

Early versions of parts 1 and 2 "The Art of Alice Teichert in Three Stages" appeared in *Open Letter*, Eleventh Series, No. 2: Summer 2001.

"What's in a Name" first appeared on Rob McLennan's blogspot, 2014.

The essays in this book were gathered in appreciation of those creative thinkers who change the landscape as they pass through.

Many thanks to my first reader, Jerry Tostevin. Also to Beverley Daurio, Ellie Nichol, Kim Ondaatje, Alice Teichert, Eugenia Sojka, Annalisa Goldoni, Margaret Christakos, Brian Dedora, David Bentley, Rob McLennan, and the friend who suggested I see the film, *We Have a Pope*.

www.ingramcontent.com/pod-product-compliance
Lightning Source LLC
Chambersburg PA
CBHW020647220526
45464CB00001B/326